Echos of Culture in the Corporate Environment

Echos of Culture in the Corporate Environment

Culture's influence on; Business negotiations,
Communication, Creativity, Employees,
and Buying Behavior

Ashraf Haggag

ISBN: 1546578528
ISBN-13: 9781546578529
Library of Congress Control Number: 2017909367
CreateSpace Independent Publishing Platform
North Charleston, South Carolina

Contents

Introduction

After delivering the final manuscript of my previous book *No Place to Stand Alone* to my publisher, I went for a short vacation, hoping to take a break and clear my mind from almost a year of continuous hard work on a daily basis. To my amazement, when I returned, I couldn't resist the strong inner desire to rush back to the office to begin drafting the outline of my new book, *Decision-Making Process in Different Cultures*. The concept of this book occupied my mind endlessly and pushed me to think about how the cultural differences among nations can affect and influence the decision-making processes in the corporate environment. Especially intriguing to me was the extent to which our mental activity, influenced by these cultural differences, plays an integral part in planning and decision-making at a vast range of levels, including budget planning, policy making, et cetera. People and organizations all over the world are engaged daily in these activities. The underlying cross-cultural differences in the decision-making process can contribute greatly to efficiency in cross-cultural communications and conflict resolution. Without the significant support of those close to me, this book would certainly not exist. I was truly blessed to have the extraordinarily dedicated support of these people. They challenged me to create and complete the final manuscript. I hope the contents will be enjoyable to my readers but also a road map to understanding the cultures of different nations and how they affect behavior and decision-making.

Enjoy the read.

One

The Definition of Culture

WHAT IS CULTURE?

The word *culture* is a notoriously difficult term to define. Most of the difficulty in understanding the concept of culture stems from the different usages of the term. However, look at the following definitions and consider the characteristics of culture that each draws attention to:

1. Culture is a complex topic that includes knowledge, beliefs, art, morals, law, customs, and habits acquired by a society.
2. Culture consists of patterns, explicit and implicit, of and for behavior acquired and transmitted by symbols constituting the distinctive achievements of human groups. The essential core of culture consists of traditional ideas, especially the values attached to them.

3. Culture consists of the derivatives of the experience of populations, more or less organized, that are learned or created by individuals, including those images or their embodiments and interpretations transmitted from past generations or contemporaries.

4. Culture is the collective programming of the mind that distinguishes the members of one group or category of people from another.

5. Culture is the set of attitudes, values, beliefs, and behaviors shared by a group of people but different for each individual, communicated from one generation to the next.

6. Culture is the hazy set of basic assumptions and values and orientation to life, beliefs, policies, procedures, and behavioral conversations that are shared by a group of people and that influence each member's behavior and his or her interpretation of the meaning of other people's behavior.

SOME KEY CHARACTERISTICS OF CULTURE

1. Culture is manifested at different layers of depth.
When analyzing the culture of a particular group or organization, it is important to identify three fundamental levels at which culture manifests itself:

- Observable artifacts
- Values
- Basic underlying assumptions

2. Culture affects behavior and interpretations of behavior.
Although certain aspects of culture are physically visible, their meanings are invisible. Their cultural meaning lies in the way these practices are interpreted by the insiders.

For example, a gesture such as the ring gesture (thumb and forefinger touching) may be interpreted as a conveying agreement, approval, or acceptance in the United States, the United Kingdom, and Canada but as an insult or obscene gesture in several Mediterranean countries. Similarly, choice of clothing can be interpreted differently by different groups of people in terms of indication of wealth, ostentation, and so on.

3. Culture can be differentiated from both universal human nature and unique individual personality.
Culture is learned, not inherited. It derives from one's social environment, not from one's genes. Culture should be distinguished from human nature on one side and from individual personality on the other.

Human nature is what all human beings have in common from Egyptian professors to the Turkish aborigines. The human ability to feel fear, anger, love, joy, sadness, and the need to associate with others is universal.

On the other hand, the personality of an individual is a uniquely personal set of mental programs that is not shared with any other human being. It is based on traits that are partly inherited with the individual's unique set of genes and

3

partly learned by the influence of collective programming (culture).

4. Culture influences biological process.
The great majority of our conscious behavior is acquired through learning and interacting with other members of our culture. Even those responses to our purely biological needs are frequently influenced by our culture.

For example, people share a biological need for food. Therefore, all people eat, but what we eat, how often we eat, how much we eat, with whom we eat, and according to what set of rules we eat are regulated at least in part by our culture.

5. Culture is associated with social groups.
Culture is shared by or more people. Everyone belongs to a number of different groups and categories of people at the same time. People unavoidably carry several layers of mental programming within themselves, corresponding to the different levels of culture:

- A national level according to one's country
- A gender level according to whether one was born as a girl or a boy
- A generation level that separates parents and children
- A role category: parent, son, daughter, teacher, student
- A social class level associated with educational opportunities and with the one's occupation or profession

6. Culture is both an individual and a social construct.
Culture is as much an individual psychological construct as it is a global social construct.

Individual differences in culture can be observed among people in the degree to which they adopt and engage in the attitudes, values, beliefs, and behavior that by consensus constitute their culture. If you act in accordance with those values or behaviors, then that culture resides in you. If you don't share those values or behaviors, then you don't share that culture.

7. Culture is always both socially and psychologically distributed in a group, and so the figuration of a culture's features will always be hazy.
Culture is a hazy concept in that group members are unlikely to share identical sets of attitudes, beliefs, and so on. The assumption that culture is uniformly distributed is unwarranted for two types of reasons:

- Sociogenic (related to social groups and institutions)
- Psychogenic (related to cognitive and affective processes characteristic of individuals)

8. Culture has both universal and distinctive elements.
Humans have largely overlapping biologies and live in fairly similar social structures and physical environments, which create similarities in the way they form their culture, but within the framework of similarities, there are differences.

9. Culture is learned.
Culture is learned from the people you interact with as you are socializing. Watching how adults react and talk to new babies is an excellent way to see the actual symbolic transmission of culture among people.

If two babies were born at exactly the same time in two different parts of the world, they may be thought to respond to physical and social stimuli in very different ways. For example, some babies are thought to smile at strangers while others are thought to smile only in very specific circumstances.

In some parts of the world, most children are asked from a very early age to make decisions about what they want to do and what they prefer, while in many other cultures, a parent would never ask a child what he or she wants to do but would simply tell the child what to do.

10. Culture is subject to gradual change.
The culture of any society is a type of snapshot view of a particular time. An individual who is witnessing and experiencing a certain situation in certain time would not find exactly the same situation several years later.

There are no cultures that remain completely static year after year.

11. Culture is a descriptive not an evaluative concept.
The interpretation of culture is often linked with terms and concepts such as *civilized*, *well educated*, *refined* or *cultured* and is associated with the results of refinements such as art, music, et cetera. However, our notion of culture is not something exclusive to certain members; rather, it relates to the whole of society. Moreover, it is not value laden. It's not that some cultures are advanced and some are backward or that some are civilized and polite while others are coarse and rude. Rather, they are similar to or different from one another.

CULTURE AND RELATED TERMS

1. Culture and nation
In our everyday language, people commonly treat *culture* and *nation* as equivalent terms.

Some nations are predominantly inhabited by one culture group, but most nations contain multiple cultures within their boundaries. Therefore, *nation* is a political term referring to a government and a set of formal and legal mechanisms that have been established to regulate the political behavior of its people.

2. Culture and race
Race commonly refers to genetic or biologically based similarities among people who are distinguishable and unique and functions to separate one group of people from another.

3. Culture and ethnicity

Ethnicity is a term that is used to refer to a wide variety of groups who might share a language, historical origins, religion, and identification with a common cultural system.

The nature of the relationship of group ethnicity to its culture will vary greatly, depending on a number of other important characteristics.

4. Culture and identity

Culture is not the same as identity. Identities consist of people's answers to the question "Where do I belong?" They are based on mutual images and emotions linked to the outer layers of the individual but not to the values.

Populations that fight one another on the basis of their differently felt identities may very well share same values.

Two

Introduction to the Culture of Europe

The culture of Europe might better be described as the sequence of overlapping cultures of Europe. Whether it be a question of West as opposed to East, Catholicism and Protestantism as opposed to Eastern Orthodoxy, or Christianity as opposed to Islam, many have claimed to identify cultural cracks across the continent.

Europe has been the source of many cultural innovations and movements, such as humanism, that have consequently been spread across the globe. The classical ideas of the Renaissance influenced the development of art and literature far beyond the borders of the continent.

Europe is divided into four conventional cultural areas: the Atlantic Fringe, the Plain, the Mediterranean area, and the Alpine area. Since the increase in modernization in the twentieth century, these areas are not often spoken of. However, the lifestyles of the people in these areas in the past helped shape the way people in the same places live today. The types of crops produced has also not changed very much from past to present. Each region has its own unique foods, customs, and ideas of what is important to daily life.

Religion

Since the spread of Christianity through Europe in the early years AD, Christianity has remained Europe's major religion. Christianity is divided into different branches—Orthodox, Protestant, and Catholic—and depending on the beliefs of different regions, people adopted them. Judaism is also practiced in Europe, and the religion of Sunni Islam is practiced in Turkey and some southern parts of Europe.

Languages

Language is paramount to culture, and Europe has a widespread variety of languages, with most countries having at least one official language. Russian is the large-scale language in Europe, followed by German. Many regional languages are also spoken, some enjoying a level of official status or recognition. Other minority languages are also spoken. The diversity on such a small territory is renowned. The European Union uses twenty official languages, which all have the same standing. The cost of translation is so great that the official language of the Union is an ongoing debate, since many

MEPs are bilingual, and most languages have a great level of prestige.

Most languages in Europe belong to the Indo-European language lineage. This lineage is divided into a number of branches, including Roman, Germanic, Baltic, Slavic, Albanian, Celtic, Armenian, and Hellenic (Greek). The Uralic languages, which include Hungarian, Finnish, and Estonian, also have a significant presence in Europe.

Three

The Effect of Culture on the European Persona and Traits

3A. THE CULTURAL IDENTITY OF ITALY

Culture

I talian culture is steeped in the arts, family, architecture, music, and food. Home of the Roman Empire and a major heart of the Renaissance, the Italian peninsula and its culture have flourished for centuries. Here is a brief overview of Italian customs and traditions.

Art

The artistic traditions of Italy have their origins in the ancient Roman Empire, which was rooted in Rome and the Italian peninsula. The classical tradition of ancient Greece and Rome has been present in Italian art throughout its history. Its two greatest and most influential periods—Renaissance and Baroque—relied strongly on the style and ideals of classical art. For centuries, artists have traveled to Italy to study both monuments from Roman times and the work of the great Italian masters of the Renaissance and Baroque eras.

Artists visiting Italy also enjoy painting and drawing the pictur-esque countryside and cities immersed in intense Mediterranean sunlight. Some artists specialize in Italianate subjects.

Before its federation in 1871, Italy was made up of many small independent city-states. The most powerful were Venice, Florence, Naples, and the Papal States centered in Rome. Different styles of art and architecture developed in each city. The major patrons of art in the cities were their wealthy ruling families. These included the Medici in Florence, the Gonzagas in Mantua, and the Farnese and Barberini in Rome. The most dominant art patrons in Italy were the ambitious popes of the Roman Catholic Church. They commissioned the leading architects and artists of the time to build and decorate their churches and palaces.

Architecture

The subject of architecture in Italy exactly makes one think of classical buildings such as the Colosseum in Rome, the Pantheon, or the Piazza of San Marco in Venice. Around the turn of the twentieth century, prominent Italian architects looked to find a national language and personal identity within the many pillars of the modernist movement while under the rule of a fascist government. However, the late twentieth and twenty-first centuries have seen a growing trend toward revitalizing cities with modern architecture and urban planning in Italy. Many famous architects, both Italian (Renzo Piano, Carlo Scarpa, Aldo Rossi) and international (Rem Koolhaas [the Netherlands], Zaha Hadid [Iraq], Richard Meier [the United States]), have designed buildings of note.

Despite Italy's already-healthy tourism industry, various cities have been tempted to commission star architect to design iconic buildings.

Literature

An example of Italian literature is the tradition of dialect lyric poetry performed in Occitan, which reached Italy by the end of the twelfth century. In 1230, the Sicilian School was notable for being the first style in standard Italian. Dante Alighieri, one of the most famous Italian poets, is notable for his *Divine Comedy*. Petrarch did classical research and wrote lyric poetry. Renaissance humanism developed during the fourteenth and the beginning of the fifteenth centuries. Humanists sought to create a citizenry able to speak and write with fluency and clarity. Early humanists, such as Petrarch, were great collectors of antique manuscripts. Lorenzo de Medici shows the influence of Florence on the Renaissance. Leonardo da Vinci wrote a treatise on painting. The development of the drama in the fifteenth century was very great.

The core characteristic of the era following the Renaissance is that it perfected the Italian character of its language. Niccolò Machiavelli and Francesco Guicciardini were the chief originators of the science of history. Pietro Bembo was an influential figure in the development of the Italian language and an influence on the sixteenth-century revival of interest in the works of Petrarch.

THE EFFECT OF ITALIAN CULTURE ON THE ITALIAN PERSONA AND TRAITS

The most famous factors of Italian culture are its art, music, style, and iconic food. Italy was the birthplace of opera, and for many generations, the language of opera was Italian, irrespective of the nationality of the composer. Popular tastes in drama in Italy have long favored comedy; the improvisational style known as the commedia dell'arte began in Italy in the midsixteenth century and is still performed today. Before being exported to France, the famous ballet dance genre also originated in Italy.

The main religion in Italy is Roman Catholic, and there are more Catholic churches per capita in Italy than in any other country. Although church attendance is relatively low, the Church itself remains influential; many office buildings have a cross or a religious article in the lobby.

Each day of the year has at least one patron saint associated with it. Children are named after a particular saint and celebrate their saint's day as if it were their own birthday.

The Church promulgates hierarchy, which can be seen in all Italian relationships. They respect and defer to those who are older, those who have achieved a level of business success, and those who come from well-connected families.

Personality
Some Italian personality traits, although broad and often stereotypical generalizations, include chattiness, fashion consciousness, sexuality, complacency, and intense individualism. In practice, this individualism often results in tight-knit communities and a generally suspicious attitude toward government. This is thought to have developed over centuries of foreign invasion.

Work etiquette
When setting up a meeting, the norm in most businesses and industries is to contact the client by e-mail or fax, followed by

a phone call, depending on the client's response, to arrange the initial meeting. In the Italian business environment, connections and networking are invaluable, and most business negotiations take place as a result of connections or through introductions by someone who is known and trusted. These connections and networking are extremely useful in setting up a meeting.

In the majority of industries, business meetings tend to take place in the morning or in the early afternoon. Italians, like most southern European people, are relationship oriented. They usually prefer to establish direct relationships, even superficially, before getting down to business. The establishment of a climate of trust and respect is as important as the exchange of information about a specific business proposal.

Meetings are a way to get a deeper and common understanding of an issue rather than forming the definitive part of a decision-making process, so in this sense, they are more exploratory and analysis oriented than decision oriented. The goal of early contact and particularly of the first meeting is to provide all the information needed regarding a proposal and, in particular, to establish a reciprocal climate of trust and respect.

Perception of others
Italians tend to be intrinsically curious about people from other cultures, although some project an attitude of suspicion toward certain foreigners. When it comes to their European

neighbors, many Italians cherish deep-seated animosity and have no qualms about telling you so. For example you may hear someone say, "The French don't like us, therefore we don't like them." Immigrants are given similar treatment. Unlike other European nations, Italy openly denied immigration to desperate Albanians and North Africans, and they make no effort to hide their contempt for immigrants who have been allowed in. Despite their feelings toward immigrants, Italians tend to be charming toward incoming tourists.

Patriotism

Italians have never been especially patriotic. Just over half the population say they are proud to be Italian, according to recent studies. Less than half the population can identify the colors of their national flag.

Italy, long a country of different national states, was unified in 1870 with the capture of Rome and the stifling of papal influence outside the Vatican. After World War II, "Il Canto degli Italiani" ("The Song of the Italians") was provisionally chosen as the national anthem. It was made official only in 2012.

Punctuality

Punctuality in Milan usually amounts to lateness of around twenty minutes. In Rome, it's half an hour, and in the south, it's around forty-five minutes. The exception may occur in a fixed-hours factory or office environment. It is therefore required that an outsider adapts and is prepared to wait from fifteen to forty-five minutes before the Italian counterpart arrives.

3B. THE CULTURAL IDENTITY OF GERMANY

Culture

The culture and traditions in Germany have been present for centuries. Despite troubles in the past, Germany's bountiful heritage still speaks through its art, architecture, literature, and cuisine. The customs and traditions are established upon punctuality, discipline, and efficiency. Below are some of the customs everyone is expected to follow in the country.

Art and architecture

The art and architecture in Germany reflect the strong cultural and historic influences in the country. The churches, palaces, universities, and many other buildings and monuments across Germany display the bountiful creations and designs of their artists and architects, who emerged during the time when much of Germany was under Roman rule.

After the Romans left the nation, other architectural styles came forth, like the French Gothic (Cologne Cathedral), German-influenced Gothic (Church of Saint Sebald in Nuremberg), Baroque (Residenz in Würzburg), and the contemporary Bauhaus style (Jewish Museum in Berlin).

Literature

Literature in the German language has undergone many changes since the Middle Ages. Through time, it has found influences in the old German traditions, then the literary scenario in Europe, and later political situations, especially during the Nazi regime.

Prominent literary works in German include *Grimm's Fairy Tales* by Jacob and Wilhelm Grimm; *Tristan und Isolde* by Gottfried von Strassburg; *Essais de Théodicée sur la Bonte de Dieu, la Liberte de l'Homme, et l'Origine du Mal* (*Theodicy: Essays on the Goodness of God, the Freedom of Man, and the Origin of Evil*) by Gottfried Wilhelm Leibniz; *Sprach Zarathustra* (*Thus Spoke Zarasthustra*) by Friedrich Nietzsche; and numerous others in a variety of genres and themes. Through 2013, German writers won thirteen Nobel Prizes in Literature, the last being Herta Muller in 2009.

THE EFFECT OF GERMAN CULTURE ON THE GERMAN PERSONA AND TRAITS

Germany has a profound history and has been a major participant in Europe's past. From this derives a culture that is filled with meaningful customs and traditions, celebrated holidays and events, and myths and folktales. Germans take immense pride in their traditional national celebrations whether they are patriotic, such as *Tag der deutschen Einheit* (Day of German Unity); religiously based, such as *Allerheiligen* (All Saints) and *Allerseelen* (All Souls); well-known holidays such as *Weihnachten* (Christmas) and *Ostern* (Easter); more personal events, such as weddings, birthdays, and funerals; or large public events like the Oktoberfest.

Germany has a modern, liberal, and globalized society, preserving a high living standard. The people of Germany highly appreciate education and family.

Personality

The Germans have a passion for work and may be considered as some of the hardest-working people on the planet. Germans have a reputation for being diligent and creative workers and have a much-used saying: "*Wenn schon, denn schon.*" Interpreted in English, this means that if something is worth doing at all, it is worth doing right.

To the outsider, it seems that the Germans never do something halfway. They are experts in organization and give great attention to detail. The negative implication here, of course, is that they are perfectionists and anxious about detail. They are orderly, and everything is expected to go by the rules. Punctuality is another byproduct: the trains are always on time, and woe be to the person who is late for a meeting with a German.

Work etiquette

For those doing business in Germany, it is essential to appreciate that business etiquette is of great importance to your German counterpart. Germany is a nation that is strongly individualistic and demands the utmost respect at all times; therefore, the highest of standards are expected.

In several respects, Germans can be considered the masters of planning. This is a culture that prizes forward thinking and conscious of what they will be doing at a specific time on a specific day. The German thought process is extremely thorough, with each aspect of a project being examined in great detail. Careful planning in one's business and personal life provides a sense of security. Most aspects of German living and working are defined and regulated by structure: for example, through laws, rules, and regulations, which are evident in all economic, political, and even social spheres. Rules and regulations allow people to know what is expected so that they can plan their lives accordingly. Germans believe that maintaining clear lines of demarcation between people, places, and things is the best way to lead a structured and ordered life. In German business culture, this is reflected in the adherence to prescribed business rules resulting in a low amount of flexibility and spontaneity in attitudes and values.

Perception of others

Two-thirds of Germans believe immigrants have caused serious problems for the country's social services and schools. The poll—commissioned by the respected Bertelsmann Foundation think tank—shows two out of three people mention that immigrants are an "extra burden" on the country's social services system.

Almost 90 percent of respondents demanded that immigrants adapt to German culture and seek out a good relationship with the Germans among whom they are living. Fully 96 percent thought that learning German should be made mandatory. Rising neo-Nazism and a long-held belief among mostly elder Germans that their country is not a country for immigrants have contributed to the image abroad of the place as unwelcoming to new residents.

Two-thirds of the people quizzed in the survey also believe that immigrants are a source of conflict with the native German nationals and cause problems with schools and the education of their own children.

Patriotism

More than six decades after the end of World War II, Germans still have a pathological fear of patriotism. Flying the flag is still an indiscretion. While cities like Washington, London, and Lisbon greatly enjoy a little flag-flying patriotism, Berlin shies away from its tricolor flag. Almost no German corporation flies a flag outside its headquarters, like British banks in the City do. In summary, national pride, especially when it comes to publicly displaying a love or even a mild affinity for Germany, is still simply unmentionable.

Punctuality

Germans are most contented when they can organize and categorize their world into controllable units. Time, therefore, is managed carefully, and calendars, schedules, and agendas must be respected. Trains arrive and leave on time to the minute, projects are carefully scheduled, and organizational charts are meticulously detailed. Germans are exceptionally punctual, and even a few minutes delay can displease. If you are going to be even slightly late, call ahead and explain your situation. Being five to ten minutes early for important appointments is the minimum requirement.

3C. THE CULTURAL IDENTITY OF FRANCE

Culture

France has a rich and diverse culture known for its art, architecture, music, language, cuisine, and of course fashion. The cultural heritage of France dates back thousands of years and is as old as the country itself.

The French population has very diverse origins, contributing to the evolution of a cosmopolitan culture. France is home to people with various ethnic backgrounds including Celts, Romans, Germans, Russians, Asians, Africans, North Americans, and other recent immigrants.

The people of France are known internationally for their sophisticated approach to life, merged with a great interest in style, fashion, and appearance. France has been an important cultural center of the world for many centuries, with Paris being the cultural hub. Even now, France contributes greatly to the fashion culture of the world.

Art

French art is a formation of the visual and plastic arts (architecture, woodwork, textiles, and ceramics) originating from the geographical area of France

Modern France was the main center for the European art of the Upper Paleolithic, then left many megalithic monuments, and there were several impressive finds of ancient art in the Iron Age.

The Gallo-Roman period left a distinctive territorial style of sculpture, and the region around the modern Franco-German border led the empire in the mass production of delicately decorated ancient Roman pottery, which was exported to Italy and elsewhere on a large scale.

France can reasonably be said to have been a pioneer in the development of Romanesque and Gothic art before the Italian Renaissance led to Italy becoming the main source of stylistic developments. This continued until the age of Louis XIV, when France largely regained this role, retaining it until the midtwentieth century.

Architecture
Architecture ranks high among France's many achievements. Signs of the special importance of architecture in France were the founding of the Academy of Architecture in 1671, the first such establishment anywhere in Europe, and the establishment in 1720 of the Prix de Rome in architecture.

Literature
Literature written in French by citizens of other nations such as Belgium, Switzerland, Canada, Senegal, Algeria, Morocco, et cetera is referred to as Francophone literature. As of 2006, French writers have been awarded more Nobel Prizes in Literature than novelists, poets, and essayists of any other country. France itself ranks first on the list of Nobel Prizes in Literature by country.

For French people, French literature has been an object of national pride for centuries, and it has been one of the most influential components of the literature of Europe.

The French language is a romance dialect derived from Latin and in large amounts influenced principally by Celtic and Frankish. Emerging in the eleventh century, literature written in medieval French was one of the oldest vernacular (non-Latin) literatures in Western Europe and it became a key source of literary themes in the middle Ages across the continent.

THE EFFECT OF FRENCH CULTURE ON THE FRENCH PERSONA AND TRAITS

Personality
French people are not impolite as such. They certainly have a unique way about them, and they are very direct and matter-of-fact. While British people tend to skirt around a subject if it helps them be more polite, French people are more willing to express displeasure or impatience.

But it's not all a one-way barrage of negativity. French people can also be very nice and will give praise when praise is due. It's more about upfront honesty and directness.

Work etiquette
French people would much rather carry out business in French. If you can't speak French, then at least learn a few

key phrases and perhaps learn how to apologize for not speaking French—it may help you build some foundations. Appointments are usually necessary and should be made up to two weeks in advance. Meetings are normally for discussing issues in depth, rather than for making decisions. And don't exaggerate anything—French people aren't overly fond of overstatement, especially in business.

Perception of others
This is where France's attitude of rudeness may arise. Unless you make an effort to speak the local lingo, French people may not be inclined to be overly friendly. Paris can be particularly bad about this, because of the large number of tourists. With large immigrant populations arriving from the north of Africa over the past half-century, some tensions have arisen. There have been a number of riots in recent years, particularly around neighborhoods with large immigrant populations. Many believe that the riots were sparked by rising anger at discrimination and racism, particularly by the police.

Patriotism
French people are quite proud of being French and believe France to be best at most things—particularly when talking about culture, intellectualism, and food! France is very self-reliant, and the general feeling is that the French way is the best way. Within France, there is a bit of a north/south divide, which is mostly good-spirited, but you often get a sense that there is genuine emotion behind a verbal condemnation of

another region. And people in Paris think everyone outside Paris is parochial.

Punctuality

In France it is essential to ensure that you make appointments for both business and social occasions. It is not acceptable in France to drop in on someone unannounced, and such conduct will be taken as an act of rudeness, whatever the occasion. While you should strive to be punctual, you will not be considered late should you arrive ten minutes after the scheduled time.

Punctuality is treated quite casually in France, although there are some regional differences; the further south you go, the more casual the approach to time is. The French have a very relaxed attitude when attending appointments themselves, so do not be surprised to find your French colleague arriving fairly late. The French consider this a prerogative, so do not expect any apologies, but as ever it will depend who you are dealing with. However, staying late at the office is common, especially for individuals in more senior positions.

3D. THE CULTURAL IDENTITY OF RUSSIA

Culture
Russian culture has a vast history and can affirm a long tradition in many aspects of the arts, especially literature, philosophy, classical music, ballet, architecture, and animation, all of which had considerable influence on world culture.

Russia was also strongly influenced by the culture of Western Europe, since the reforms of Peter the Great. For two centuries Russian culture largely developed in the general context of European culture rather than pursuing its own unique ways. However, the situation changed in the twentieth century when the communist ideology became a major factor in the culture of the Soviet Union.

Russian cultural heritage is classified seventh in the nation brands index, based on careful and detailed research conducted mainly among Western countries and the Far East. Because of Russia's the late involvement in modern globalization and the international community, many aspects of Russian culture (i.e., the arts) remain largely unknown to many people.

Russian literature is thought to be among the most influential and developed in the world, as it includes some of the world's most famous literary works. Russian literary history dates back to the tenth century. In the early nineteenth century, a modern tradition emerged, producing some of the greatest writers of all time. This golden age of Russian poetry began with Alexander Pushkin, who is considered the founder of modern Russian literature and has been described as the Russian Shakespeare or the Russian Goethe. It continued with more giants, including Mikhail Lermontov, Nikolai Nekrasov, Anton Chekhov, Leo Tolstoy and many others.

Tolstoy and Dostoyevsky in particular were the titanic figures, to the point that many literary critics have described one or the other as the greatest novelist ever.

Classical music is well known for having the best orchestras in the world and is known by its titans (including Peter Tchaikovsky, Sergei Rachmaninov, and Alfred Schnittke).

Russian ballet with its rich traditions and famous dancers is the most important cultural symbol of Russia, and Russian classical ballet schools are considered to be the best in the world.

Classical ballet came to Russia in the eighteenth century. By the end of the nineteenth century, its national school of ballet had been formed. It has concentrated the achievements of the best ballet schools of the world and enriched Russia with national dance traditions.

Sergei Diaghilev had great significance for the Russian music and dance arts with his Russian seasons project in the early twentieth century.

Architectural monuments are cultural symbols in Russia. The development of Russian culture is indestructibly linked with the religious tradition; Orthodox Christianity came into ancient Russia in the tenth century. Churches, cathedrals, and monasteries constructed in different centuries reflect the spirituality of Russia.

The Hermitage, Russian Museum, Marini Theater in Saint Petersburg and Bolshoi Theater are recognized as significant symbols of Russia's culture.

THE EFFECT OF RUSSIAN CULTURE ON THE RUSSIAN PERSONA AND TRAITS

Personality

Older generations of Russians, although for the most part well educated, hardworking, and disciplined, are the product of the communist system, in which workers were not rewarded for personal incentives or punished for being unproductive.

Not having been raised to get ahead and to amass personal fortunes, they may respect these traits in foreigners but generally abhor them in their Russian colleagues. You may hear the expression "Initiative is punishable" from members of the older generations, and it can be difficult to convince them that personal initiative and doing your own thinking are necessities in the new Russia.

The attitude of younger generations is, for the most part, very different. Achievement in the work place is highly regarded; you can find highly trained young Russians who, on top of having an excellent education, speak fluent English and other foreign languages.

Work etiquette
In Russia the types of businesses you may deal with can range from a new-style entrepreneur to an old-school Soviet bureaucrat. It is difficult to do business in Russia without the help of a local "connection." To ease this, small gifts are often a good idea when doing business in Russia. Presents should symbolize the status of your company and the importance of the impending business deal, preferably items characteristic of your local area or displaying the company logo.

Patience is important with Russians; negotiations can many times be slow. As the Russian proverb states, "Do not hurry to reply, but hurry to listen." Russians don't usually make an instant decision in a meeting; generally, a certain amount of deliberation is done in private afterward.

Perception of others
Although Russians have a history of not being warm to Western powers, they claim to be passionately interested in the rest of the world. There has always been a tendency in Russia for foreigners to be treated differently than the native people. Foreign tourists have been allowed into museums

ahead of huge lines of Russians who may have traveled just as far, or farther, to be there. Many Russian cities have tourist hotels that were built solely for the use of foreign visitors, and—notoriously—until the recent change of regime, Russians were not allowed into the premier hotels in Moscow or Saint Petersburg unless a foreign friend met them at the door and escorted them in past the doorman.

Patriotism

Most Russians define patriotism simply as "love of the motherland." Though there is much disagreement over what this means in practice, most see patriotism as both political and intensely personal. For instance, the one event unequivocally associated with patriotism—the state-sponsored celebration of Victory Day (May 9)—carries such resonance in large part because the Soviet Union's massive losses in World War II left their mark on virtually every family. Underscoring the primary nature of the familial tie, interview and focus group participants cited the "Immortal Regiment" in Victory Day parades (in which participants carry pictures of relatives who fought in war) as conveying real emotional power for both observers and participants. By contrast, opinions divided over the government's exploitation of wartime symbols like the orange-and-black Saint George's ribbons in other contexts.

Punctuality

Russia is a polychronic culture: in other words, people tend to be flexible in the organization of their priorities, and attitudes toward punctuality are relaxed. Polychronic cultures often feel it is more efficient to do several things at once; therefore, meetings may not follow a linear agenda and may be interrupted by phone calls or people coming in. As a foreigner, you are expected to be on time to all business appointments. However, social events are more relaxed, and being up to thirty minutes late is acceptable. Patience is highly valued in the Russian society. Try not to be mad when a colleague arrives late, and do not expect an apology. They may simply be testing your patience.

Ashraf Haggag

3E. THE CULTURAL IDENTITY OF GREAT BRITAIN

Culture

The United Kingdom is made up of four countries: England, Scotland, Wales, and Northern Ireland. It is important to be aware not only of these geographical distinctions, but also of the strong sense of identity and nationalism felt by the populations of these four nations.

The terms *English* and *British* do not mean the same thing. *British* denotes someone who is from England, Scotland, Wales, or Northern Ireland. *English* refers to people from England. People from Scotland are *Scots*, from Wales *Welsh*, and from Northern Ireland *Irish*. Be sure not to refer to someone who is Welsh, Scots, or Northern Irish as English.

Formerly a very homogenous society, since World War II, Britain has become increasingly diverse. It has accommodated large immigrant populations, particularly from its former colonies such as India, Pakistan, and the West Indies. The mixture of ethnic groups and cultures makes it difficult to define Britishness nowadays, and a debate rages within the nation as to what now really constitutes being a Briton.

Arts and architecture

Throughout England's history, its art has been influenced by that of the rest of Europe. But England has also made its own unique contributions to world art. In architecture, the English version of the Gothic style produced churches of great beauty; later English architects captured the spirit of the Italian Renaissance style and transformed it to suit English needs.

Perhaps most influential was the great era of English painting that began in the 1700s. This period set new standards for landscape painting and established watercolor as an important artistic medium. In the 1800s and 1900s, individual English artists continued to have an impact on international movements and trends.

THE EFFECT OF BRITISH CULTURE ON THE BRITISH PERSONA AND TRAITS

The culture of the United Kingdom is influenced by its history as a developed island country, a liberal democracy, and a major power; its predominantly Christian religious life; and its four countries—England, Northern Ireland, Scotland, and Wales— each of which has distinct customs, cultures, and symbolism. The wider culture of Europe has also influenced British culture, and humanism, Protestantism, and representative democracy developed from broader Western culture. Literature, music, film, art, theater, media, television, philosophy, architecture, and education are important aspects of British culture.

Sports are an important part of British culture; numerous sports originated in the country, including soccer. The UK has been described as a "cultural superpower," and London has been described as a world cultural capital.

The Industrial Revolution, which started in the UK, had a profound effect on the socioeconomic and cultural conditions of the world. As a result of the British Empire, significant British influence can be observed in the language, law, culture, and institutions of a wide assortment of countries, including Australia, Canada, India, the Republic of Ireland, New Zealand, Nigeria, Pakistan, South Africa, the United States, and the English-speaking Caribbean nations. These countries are sometimes collectively known as the Anglosphere and are among Britain's closest allies. In turn, the empire also influenced British culture.

The cultures of England, Scotland, Wales, and Northern Ireland are diverse and have varying degrees of overlap and distinctiveness.

Personality
The British are a diverse, multinational, and multicultural society, with strong regional accents, expressions, and identities. The social structure of the United Kingdom has changed radically since the nineteenth century, with a decline in religious observance; enlargement of the middle class; and particularly since the 1950s, increased ethnic diversity.

British people live in the United Kingdom—in England, Scotland, Wales, or Northern Ireland. British people are either English, Scottish, Welsh, or Irish (from Northern Ireland only).

The British are said to be timid in manners, dress, and speech. They are famous for their politeness, self-discipline, and especially their sense of humor. British people have a strong sense of humor that sometimes can be hard for foreigners to understand.

Britain is a country of mixed cultures. London has the largest nonwhite population of any European city, and more than 250 languages are spoken there. Therefore, not all British people are white or Christian.

Work etiquette

Time is exceptionally valued in the UK corporate world, with wasted time being considered a wasted resource. Punctuality is therefore a crucial trait, and almost everyone will either arrive on time or a few minutes early for meetings. If you arrive a couple of minutes late for a meeting, it is usually enough to apologize to the room, but if you are going to be later than that, it is polite to call the organizers in advance to warn them and apologize. Most meetings have specific objectives or topics of discussion, often indicated by the distribution of an agenda prior to the meeting itself. It is generally assumed that discussion will stick to the agenda, perhaps after an informal chat at the beginning of the meeting. If there are other issues to discuss, there may be time for AOB (any other business). Generally, topics are brought up and discussed, and then suggestions for action will be made. Business cards are often exchanged at business occasions, particularly if you are meeting a new client. It is polite to receive these gratefully, perhaps taking a second to glance at the card as a sign of respect. Not everyone will have business cards, so do not be offended if someone does not offer you theirs.

Perception of others

Attitudes toward foreigners vary greatly, depending more on the individual British person than the nationality of the foreigners. Labeling people based on stereotypes isn't a distinctly British trait. Some British have never travelled as far as Calais and regard the whole of "abroad" with a mixture of pity and fear. Others travel widely in Europe and elsewhere, know about French wine and German music, can comment wisely on the American political scene, and are keenly interested in the Far Eastern stock market. The traditional British tolerance of diversity exists alongside the less attractive tradition of insularity.

Patriotism

National identity and citizenship are not always the same thing in Great Britain or the UK.

Most white people born in Great Britain, although British citizens, do not regard themselves as British and prefer to state their national identity as English, Scottish, or Welsh. On one hand, they have historically prized individualism and been wary of the state. On the other hand, loyalty to the national community is expected, and previous generations have taken it for granted.

Punctuality

In general, the British value timekeeping for business arrangements. If you set up a meeting for two o'clock, the chances are your counterparts will arrive on time or just before. Since the British are so time conscious, sometimes you may feel their lives are very rushed. In fact, however, they are only doing their best to avoid losing time, which is valued as an economic resource. It is considered very impolite to arrive late for a business meeting. If your delay is inevitable, and you arrive late, it is usually sufficient to excuse yourself with an apology. If, however, you are running more than a few minutes late, you should call ahead to apologize and give an indication of how long you will be; in the case of a long delay that would compromise the value of attending the meeting, you should consider offering to postpone the meeting to a new time and/ or day. The busier people are, the greater the likelihood that they will have to leave for another engagement, so respecting their time is very important.

3F. THE CULTURAL IDENTITY OF SPAIN

Culture

The cultures of Spain are European cultures based on a variety of historical influences, primarily that of Ancient Rome, but also the pre-Roman Celtic and Iberian cultures and those of the Phoenicians and the Moors. In the areas of language and religion, the ancient Romans left a lasting legacy.

The subsequent course of Spanish history added other elements to the country's culture and traditions.

Muslim influences were strong during the Middle Ages. The Spanish language derives directly from Vulgar Latin, with significant lexical borrowings from Andalusian Arabic and minor influences from other languages including Basque, Iberian, Celtic, and Gothic. Another influence was the minority Jewish population in some cities. After the defeat of the Muslims during the Christian *Reconquista* period between 718 and 1492, Spain became an almost entirely Roman Catholic country. In addition, the nation's history and its Mediterranean and Atlantic environment have played significant roles in shaping its culture as well as other cultures, such as the culture of Latin America through the colonization of the Americas.

By the end of the nineteenth and twentieth centuries, the Spaniards made expressions of cultural diversity easier than they had been for the prior seven centuries. This occurred as Spain became increasingly drawn into a diverse international culture.

Spain has the third highest number of UNESCO World Heritage Sites in the world, after Italy and China, with a total of forty-five.

Art and architecture

Spain has been an important contributor to Western art and has produced many famous and influential artists including Velázquez, Goya, and Picasso.

The prehistoric art of Spain had many important periods. Spain was one of the main centers of European Upper Paleolithic art and the rock art of the Spanish Levant in subsequent periods. In the Iron Age, Northwestern Spain was a center for Celtic art, and Iberian sculpture has a distinct style, partly influenced by coastal Greek settlements. Spain was conquered by the Romans by 200 BC, and Rome was rather smoothly replaced in the fifth century AD by the Germanic Visigoths, who represented only a small ruling class who soon Christianized. The relatively few remains of Visigothic art and architecture show an attractive and distinct version of wider European trends, but the Muslim conquest of most of Spain in the eighth century was a massive disruption and transformation. Over the centuries that followed, the wealthy courts of Al-Andaluz produced many works of exceptional quality, culminating in the Alhambra in Granada, right at the end of Muslim Spain.

Architecture

Due to its historical and geographical diversity, Spanish architecture has drawn from a host of influences. Iberian architecture started to take shape in parallel with other architectures around the Mediterranean and in Northern Europe.

Toward the end of the fifteenth century, before influencing Latin America with its Colonial architecture, Spain itself experimented with Renaissance architecture, developed mostly by local architects. Spanish Baroque was distinguished by its exuberant Churrigueresque decoration and the most sober Herrerian style, both developing separately from later international influences. The Colonial style, which has lasted for centuries, still has a strong influence in Latin America.

Literature
Spanish literature is the name given to the literary works written in Spain throughout time and those by Spanish authors worldwide. Due to historic, geographic, and generational diversity, Spanish literature has known a great number of influences. Some major movements can be identified within it.

Highlights include the *Cantar de Mio Cid*, the oldest preserved Spanish *cantar de gesta* (epic poem). It is written in medieval Spanish, the ancestor of modern Spanish.

La Celestina is a book published anonymously by Fernando de Rojas in 1499. This book is considered one of the greatest in Spanish literature and traditionally marks the end of medieval literature and the beginning of the literary renaissance in Spain.

THE EFFECT OF SPANISH CULTURE ON THE SPANISH PERSONA AND TRAITS

Spanish culture is widely known for flamenco music and dance, bullfights, fantastic beaches, and lots of sunshine. It is—and has been for thousands of years—one of the cultural centers of Europe.

Spaniards cherish their free time and social lives along with their particular Spanish customs and traditions, which represent a key part of the Spanish culture. Spanish people often meet with friends in big groups to enjoy the good weather while sipping on their favorite beverage or just strolling around chatting about everything: soccer, politics, family life, work, Spanish fashion, celebrities, or television.

Personality

The main preoccupation of the Spanish is having a good time, and they have a zest for life matched by few other peoples. They take childish pleasure in making the most of everything and grasp every opportunity to make merry. The Spanish are inveterate celebrants and, when not attending a fiesta, family celebration, or impromptu party, are to be found in bars and restaurants indulging in other favorite pastimes: eating and drinking.

Work etiquette

In Spain, most companies are still hierarchically structured, although the old mind-set is changing at high speed. For instance family-owned businesses as well as most government undertakings are run in a traditional Spanish way: with strictly separated divisions and a strong hierarchical system.

However, the strong hierarchical and bureaucratic organizational culture is changing because of a growing number of young managers educated abroad and changes in Spanish society itself. Throughout the Spanish economy, individualism is predominant in management, whereas teamwork is not appreciated as much. In Spanish organizations, planning does not seem to be that important, mainly "because no one can predict the future." The strategy of an organization is the sole responsibility of the managing director or the owner of the company, who relies more on intuition than on systematic research. Meetings are merely held to give instructions to and exchange ideas with subordinates; making decisions or reaching consensus is not the key activity. Despite the changes in Spanish society, decisions are still made at senior management level, often by the senior executive alone. A modest employee is more appreciated than an assertive employee.

Spaniards have a very warm and outgoing nature and consider meals a social activity. While it is more typical for negotiations to be done within an office, it is not uncommon to celebrate afterward at a restaurant.

Perception of others
Spain can boast of having achieved the integration of more than six million immigrants in record time, without having

witnessed the appearance of xenophobic movements, becoming in this respect an exception to the European norm.

Patriotism

Spaniards are often disparaging about their compatriots from other regions. Nobody understands the Basques and their tongue twister of a language, the Galicians are derided as being more Portuguese than Spanish, and the Andalusians are scorned as backward peasants. However, the most widespread antagonism is between the cities of Madrid and Barcelona, whose inhabitants argue about everything, including the economy, sports, history, politics, culture, and language. Catalans claim that Madrileños are half African, to which they reply that it's better than being half French. However, although they're proud of their regional identity, most Spanish aren't nationalists or patriotic and have little loyalty to Spain as a whole.

Punctuality

Spain is famous for its relaxed lifestyle, siestas, and what could be called less-than-punctual timing. The country simply doesn't work in the same way that other Western countries do. However, that doesn't mean you should be late for any business meetings or appointments. Chances are that the Spanish contingent that you meet up with may be slightly delayed, which isn't seen as a big deal in Spain, but you don't want to arrive late yourself to find that they have arrived earlier—this will not go down well. The best advice would be to arrive on time, order a drink, and wait for your partners to arrive.

Ashraf Haggag

3G. THE CULTURAL IDENTITY OF GREECE

Culture

Greece is a country of great interests and diverse cultures, influenced by its location at the junction between the East and the West and by the many occupations of the Greek people throughout history.

The Greeks are particularly proud of their culture and speak of their country with an intense passion, feeling that the culture in Greece is a definition of their national and ethnic belonging. Traditions, religion, music, language, food, and wine compose the culture in Greece and constitute the basis for those who wish to visit and understand today's country.

Arts

Production, education, publicity, festivals, and national centers such as the Greek Film Center are important elements of the Greek art scene. There are provincial and municipal theaters, folklore institutes, orchestras, conservatories, dance centers, art workshops, and literary groups.

Long-standing traditions of pottery, metalworking, rug making, wood carving, and textile production have been carried forward by artisan and craft cooperatives. Many sculptors and painters are in the vanguard of contemporary European art, while others continue the tradition of Orthodox icon painting.

Music and dance are major forms of group and self-expression, and genres vary from Byzantine chants to the music of the urban working class known as *rebetika*. Distinctively Greek styles of music, dance, and instrumentation have not been displaced by the popularity of Western European and American music. Some of the most commonly used instruments are the bouzouki, the *santouri* (hammer dulcimer), the *lauto* (mandolin-type lute), the clarinet, the violin, the guitar, the *tsambouna* (bagpipe), and the *lyra* (a stringed Cretan instrument), many of which function as symbols of national or regional identity. The popular composers Mikis Theodorakis and Manos Hadjidakis have achieved international fame.

Shadow puppet plays revolving around the wily character known as Karagiozis were very popular in the late Ottoman period. Dozens of theater companies in Athens, Thessaloniki, and other areas perform contemporary works and ancient dramas in modern Greece. Films are a popular form of entertainment, and several Greek filmmakers and production companies have produced a body of melodramas, comedies, musicals, and art films.

Literature

Oral poetry and folk songs thrived even under Ottoman domination and developed into more formal, written forms as the nation-state emerged. Poets and novelists have brought contemporary national themes into alignment with the major movements in Western literature. There have been two Greek Nobel laureates: George Seferis and Odysseas Elytis.

THE EFFECT OF GREEK CULTURE ON THE GREEK PERSONA AND TRAITS

The culture of Greece has evolved over thousands of years, beginning in Mycenaean Greece, continuing most notably into Classical Greece, through the influence of the Roman Empire and its successor, the Byzantine Empire. Other cultures and states such as the Persian Empire, the Latin and Frankish states, the Ottoman Empire, the Venetian Republic, the Genoese Republic, and the British Empire have also left their influence on modern Greek culture, but historians credit the Greek War of Independence with revitalizing Greece and giving birth to a single entity for its multifaceted culture.

Personality

The Greeks see themselves as being Greek, and this is identified in a very specific yet historic way. To be Greek, one has to be a native Greek speaker and live a Greek lifestyle, no matter where one lives or what one's ethnicity is. Due to Greece's long history as a powerful nation both ruling over minorities and being ruled by foreigners, citizenship, government, and even ethnicity to a degree are features that mean little to the people included in this identity. The most important aspects of being Greek, both now and in the past, are to live and speak as the Greeks do, whether that's in Greece or abroad.

Most Greeks enjoy life, and their daily way of life is centered on family, friends, good food, perhaps a drink of two, and relaxation. However, there is also a growing pressure to work hard. Having jobs is only important to the Greeks so they can support their families and enjoy life; few Greeks have the desire to be financially wealthy, as they often define wealth in very different terms.

Work etiquette

As Greek culture revolves around eating and drinking, business is often conducted over coffee or lunch. These meetings are an integral part of developing a successful business relationship. A moderate amount of small talk usually takes place before moving to the business aspect of a meeting. It is important not to rush this along and to allow your Greek business partners to decide when they are ready to get down to business.

Good topics for small talk include general questions about a person's background, family, and career. When doing business with a company for the first time, it is not unusual for it to take several meetings before business is discussed. Greeks are generally cautious about who they do business with and want to develop a relationship of trust, getting to know a potential business partner before making any decisions.

Greek culture is grounded in negotiation and haggling. Meetings will often become loud and chaotic, and passionate debate is encouraged. In business and in life in general, Greeks have a very emotional, almost theatrical, style of communication and will often use hand gestures for emphasis. You may have to be very assertive to get your point across. This lively communication style is usually good natured, however, and should not be mistaken for aggressiveness.

Perception of others
Greeks see themselves differently than others see them. Contradictory stereotypes may complicate any resolution of the new Greek crisis. Greeks see themselves as the most hardworking Europeans, according to a 2012 Pew Research Center survey. The British, the Germans, the Spanish, the Poles, and the Czechs all see the Greeks as the least hardworking. And the Greeks see themselves as the most trustworthy of Europeans, while the French, the Germans, and the Czechs voice the view that the Greeks are the least trustworthy, according to a 2013 Pew Research survey.

Patriotism
Greeks have an intense love for their country, with 71 percent having a favorable view of their own country; only the Germans and the British are more patriotic. Also, 60 percent of Greeks think they're the most hardworking people in Europe.

Punctuality
Punctuality is not particularly important in Greece, but foreigners are expected to be on time for business meetings, even though their Greek counterparts may be late.

Four

Introduction to the Culture of Asia

The culture of Asia is diverse. The different kinds of cultural heritage of many nationalities, societies, and ethnic groups exist on the continent of Asia. The continent is commonly divided into more natural geographic and cultural sub-regions, including Central Asia, East Asia, North Asia, South Asia, Southeast Asia and West Asia. Culturally, there has been little unity or common history for many of the cultures and peoples of Asia. Asian art, music, and cuisine, as well as literature, are important parts of Asian culture. Eastern philosophy and religion—Hinduism, Taoism, Confucianism, Buddhism, Judaism, and Islam—also play major roles. One of the most complex parts of Asian culture is the relationship between traditional cultures and the Western world.

Religion

Asia is the largest and most populous continent, with a wide variety of religions. Asia was the birthplace of many religions, such as Islam, Christianity, Hinduism, Buddhism, Confucianism, Taoism, Jainism, Sikhism, and Zoroastrianism.

Languages

The languages of Asia are richly diverse. The vast majority of the people of continental Asia speak a language in one of three large language families. The first, Altaic, consists of the Turkic, Mongolian, and Manchu-Tungus (Tungusic) sub-families. The second, Sino-Tibetan, includes the Chinese and Tibeto-Burman languages. Finally, the Indo-European family consists of the Indo-Aryan, Iranian, and Slavic languages, as well as Armenian.

The peoples of peninsular and insular Asia, however, speak numerous other languages, including those in the Austroasiatic, Tai, Hmong-Mien (Miao-Yao), and Dravidian families, as well as Japanese, Korean, a vast number of Austronesian languages, and the unrelated languages lumped together within the Paleo-Siberian areal category. Also spoken on the western bounds of Asia are Arabic and Hebrew (both Afro-Asiatic languages) and the Caucasian languages.

Five

The Effect of Culture on the Asian Persona and Traits

5A. THE CULTURAL IDENTITY OF CHINA

Culture

The Chinese culture is one of the oldest and most complex cultures in the world. The culture of China has been influenced by China's long history and by its diverse ethnic groups, whose customs and traditions could vary greatly among towns, cities, and provinces. Despite its regional diversity, the Chinese culture is dominated by the Confucian value system. It has been the ethical and philosophical system in China since its foundation by Confucius two thousand years ago. It is a complex system of morals; social behavior; and political, philosophical, and quasi-religious thought that has had tremendous influence on the culture and history of China. Confucianism emphasizes self-restraint, good relationships with others, and mutuality to promote social harmony. Confucianism advocates respect for hierarchy and emphasizes loyalty to authority, family, spouse, and friends to keep society in good order. Confucianism also exhorts all people to strive to be a perfect gentleman or lady and to be humane to all people. Confucianism is embedded in people's behavior and business culture in China. Many Chinese business people attach great importance to cultivating, maintaining, and developing a personal relationship (*guanxi*) before doing business. China comprises many ethnic groups. Among them, Han Chinese is the majority ethnic group of the total population. The other ethnic groups are consequently referred to as minority ethnic groups or minorities. China is a country of religious pluralism. Religions include Buddhism, Taoism, Islam, Christianity, Judaism, and other smaller religions. Confucianism is considered by many to be a quasi religion.

Architecture

The architecture of China is as old as Chinese civilization. From every source of information—literary, graphic, exemplary—there is strong evidence that the Chinese have always enjoyed an indigenous system of construction that has retained its principal characteristics from prehistoric times to the present day.

Over the vast area from Chinese Turkistan to Japan, from Manchuria to the northern half of French Indochina, the same system of construction is prevalent, and this was the area of Chinese cultural influence. That this system of construction could perpetuate itself for more than four thousand years over such a vast territory and still remain a living architecture, retaining its principal characteristics in spite of repeated foreign invasions—military, intellectual, and spiritual—is a phenomenon comparable only to the continuity of the civilization of which it is an integral part.

Throughout the twentieth century, Western-trained Chinese architects have attempted to combine traditional Chinese designs with modern architecture. Moreover, the pressure for urban development throughout contemporary China required greater speed of construction and a higher floor-area ratio, which means that in the great cities, the demand for traditional Chinese buildings, which normally have fewer than three levels, has declined in favor of modern architecture. However, the traditional skills of Chinese architecture, including major and minor carpentry, masonry, and stonemasonry, are still applied to the construction of vernacular architecture in the vast rural area in China.

Arts

Chinese art is visual art that, whether ancient or modern, originated in or is practiced in China or by Chinese artists. The Chinese art in the Republic of China (Taiwan) and that of overseas Chinese can also be considered part of Chinese art when it is based in or draws on Chinese heritage and Chinese culture.

Early Stone Age art dates back to 10,000 BC, mostly consisting of simple pottery and sculptures. After this early period, Chinese art, like Chinese history, is typically classified by the succession of ruling dynasties of Chinese emperors, most of which lasted several hundred years.

Chinese art has arguably the oldest continuous tradition in the world and is marked by an unusual degree of continuity within, and consciousness of, that tradition, lacking an equivalent to the Western collapse and gradual recovery of classical styles.

The media that have usually been classified in the West since the Renaissance as the decorative arts are extremely important in Chinese art, and much of the finest work was produced in large workshops or factories by essentially unknown artists, especially in the area of Chinese porcelain.

Much of the best work in ceramics, textiles, and other techniques was produced over a long period by the various imperial factories or workshops. As well as being used by the court, they were distributed internally and abroad on a huge scale to demonstrate the wealth and power of the emperors.

In contrast, the tradition of ink wash painting, especially of landscapes, flowers, and birds, practiced mainly by scholar-officials and court painters, developed aesthetic values depending on the individual imagination and objective observation by the artist that are similar to those of the West, but long predated their development there. After contacts with Western art became increasingly important from the nineteenth century onward, in recent decades China has participated with increasing success in worldwide contemporary art.

THE EFFECT OF CHINESE CULTURE ON THE CHINESE PERSONA AND TRAITS

Personality
The Chinese are very conscious of face. Face is essentially respect in the community and is a crucial underpinning of society. Loss of that respect threatens the relations of individuals with almost everyone in their world and is hard to get back once lost; thus, it must be avoided at all costs. Chinese also value loyalty and stress the importance of keeping one's word. Discretion is greatly valued. It is tied to humility and not causing others to lose face.

Chinese often smile or giggle when a sensitive subject is broached or when they feel embarrassed or uncomfortable. When young Chinese are asked if they have a girlfriend or boyfriend, they usually laugh and look away. Chinese often grin when something bad has happened. Laughing loudly is often a sign of uneasiness.

Successful Chinese are often very modest. Most of China's superrich are publicity shy. They rarely grant interviews, and little is known about them. When they do talk, they tend to talk more about their two-dollar haircuts than lavish possessions. Perhaps they are reminded of the old Chinese proverb: "Fame portends trouble for men, just as fattening does a pig."

Work etiquette

The central concept of *guanxi* means *relationship network* or *connections*. This network functions on solidarity, support, and mutual aid. In the business world, to have a good *guanxi* is important to ensure minimal difficulties and frustrations. *Mianzi* or *face* is the personal mark of pride and base of one's individual reputation and social status. Saving face, losing face, and giving face are key elements in the success of businesses. To lose face is not only to be shamed but also to be deeply touched within one's soul.

Keqi, a concept based on the combination of two Chinese words—*ke* meaning *guest* and *qi* meaning *behavior*—recommends a courteous, thoughtful, and refined behavior. In business terms, it is important to show humility and modesty because expressing exaggerated claims will be seen with suspicion.

Perception of others
Chinese tend to be very formal and have an us-versus-them attitude toward outsiders. Their formality persists until one is allowed inside their group, which is something that usually takes place over time and requires following established protocol, recognizing hierarchies, and showing proper respect to achieve.

Patriotism
Chinese Communists combine patriotism with internationalism. They are at once internationalists and patriots, and their slogan is "Fight to defend the motherland against the aggressors." For them, defeatism is a crime, and to strive for victory in the War of Resistance is an inescapable duty. For only by fighting in defense of the motherland can they defeat the aggressors and achieve national liberation. And only by achieving national liberation will it be possible for the proletariat and other working people to achieve their own emancipation. The victory of China and the defeat of the invading imperialists will help the people of other countries. Thus, in wars of national liberation, patriotism is applied internationalism.

Punctuality
The Chinese view punctuality as a virtue. Arriving late is an insult and could negatively affect your relationship. When the meeting is finished, you are expected to leave before your Chinese counterparts.

5B. THE CULTURAL IDENTITY OF KOREA

Culture

Korea is a small peninsula on the Far East side of Asia. It is between China and Japan. It is connected to mainland Asia in the North and separated from China and Russia by the Yalu and Tuman Rivers. Between Korea and Japan is the East Sea. To the West between Korea and China is the Yellow Sea. Korea is roughly one thousand kilometers in length.

Korea is a divided country. At the end of World War II, Korea was divided at the 38th parallel into North Korea and South Korea. North Korea became communist, while South Korea did not. (This was based on the deal at the end of the war, dividing the country in two just as Germany had been).

North Korea is also known as the Democratic People's Republic of Korea, and South Korea is also known as the Republic of Korea. South Korea is slightly larger in geographical size, while its population is about twice the size of North Korea's.

The essence of Korean culture is harmony with order, as opposed to American mainstream culture, which stresses individualism. Influenced by Confucianism, Koreans value harmony within family, community, and society as a whole. They have strong ties to family and value education, hard work, and ambition to excel. Commonly cited virtues in traditional Korea include filial piety, respect for elders, benevolence, loyalty, trust, cooperation, reciprocity, and humility. These traditional

values are often challenged, however, by younger generations influenced by Western culture.

THE EFFECT OF KOREAN CULTURE ON THE KOREAN PERSONA AND TRAITS

Personality

Koreans are very status conscious, and their speech reflects the
hierarchical relationship among social actors. Except among
former classmates and other very close friends, adults do not
use first names to address one another. Position titles such as
professor, manager, director, and *president* are used in combination with the honorific suffix *nim* to address a social superior.

Koreans are generally courteous to the extent of being
ceremonious when they interact with social superiors but can
be very outgoing and friendly among friends and acquain-
tances of equal social status. Their behavior with strangers
in urban public situations may be characterized by indiffer-
ence and self-centeredness. Koreans appear to be rude to
strangers since they generally do not say a word when they
accidentally push or jostle other people on the streets and in
the stores, train stations, and airports. Traditional Confucian
teaching emphasizes propriety in the five sets of human relationships, which include the relations between sovereign and
subject, father and son, husband and wife, senior and junior,
and friend and friend. Confucianism still serves as the standard of moral and social conduct for many people.

Work etiquette

Koreans hold to firm Confucian traditions, which emphasize respect for education, authorities, and those who are older. Although modern Koreans may not adhere to Confucian principles as rigidly, these principles continue to underpin many customs and business practices.

Given this Confucian influence, Koreans intuitively establish hierarchical relationships based on the age, position, status, and educational background of other people relative to themselves. Do not be surprised by questions about your age, marital status, or educational background. Although these questions are considered by many to be personal in nature—and unrelated to business—they are a tool used by Korean businesspeople to place you within this hierarchical structure.

The exchange of business cards is helpful in determining rank within the hierarchical structure and allows Koreans to quickly determine their counterpart's position and title. The exchange of business cards plays an essential role in initial meetings.

For appointments, it is considered polite to arrive on time or just a few minutes early. Koreans generally keep a full schedule, which early arrivals can disrupt. Arriving late is not recommended, however, as it can be viewed as a snub by your host.

At an initial meeting, be prepared to begin with some small talk, including discussion of whether you are making your first visit to Korea and your impressions of the country, as well as your family, favorite sports (golf is a clear favorite among Koreans), and other interests.

Perception of others

Following the partition of Korea in the aftermath of the Korean War, the number of foreigners in South Korea has risen to about two million, half of them Chinese, with Americans and Vietnamese tied for second place at around one hundred fifty thousand each. North Korea remains largely ethnically homogeneous with a small Chinese expatriate community and a few Japanese migrants.

South Koreans are more open and tolerant toward foreigners and immigrants living in South Korea than we previously thought. They are, however, still defensive and protectionist toward foreign capital and cultures that compete with theirs. They are willing to engage in conflict with foreign countries to protect South Korea's interests. I attribute these attitudes to the level of perceived threat that South Koreans fear immigrants and foreign countries may pose. South Koreans tend to think immigrants living in South Korea are not a serious threat to their economy and culture because they are a small and powerless minority group. The public perception that they are a disadvantaged and mistreated group also engenders South Koreans' sympathy toward them. However, they think competition from foreign countries at the economic and cultural level is real and serious enough to weaken the local economy and culture.

Patriotism
Koreans are among the most patriotic people in the world. Their love for their country is unequaled. Outside being hard working, everything that they have achieved so far was spurred by an undying love for their country and the sheer zeal to place their country on the world map. Such attitudes deserve paean and fete.

Punctuality
Punctuality is important as it is a sign of respect, and notification of lateness is a must. However, despite needing to show punctuality, it isn't a surprise if top Korean executives arrive a few minutes late for appointments as they are extremely busy and have high pressure in their schedules.

It is also not unusual for Korean executives to cancel appointments with little or no notice. The cancellation may genuinely be due to an unexpected situation.

5C. THE CULTURAL IDENTITY OF JAPAN

Culture

Japan's geographical location has played a crucial role in its culture. Japan lies close enough to the mainland of Asia to have been strongly influenced by China. At the same time, the waters surrounding the Japanese islands long served as a barrier against invasion.

After the first migrations of people from the mainland in the faraway past, Japan successfully resisted attempts at invasion until its defeat in World War II. This water blockade also encouraged the isolation that marks periods of Japanese history.

The Japanese call their country *Nippon* or *Nihon*, which means *base of the sun*, suggesting that Japan is the land where the sun rises.

The national flag illustrates the sun—a red ball—against a white background. The Japanese emperors traced their ancestry to a sun goddess, who in turn was descended from the god Izanagi. A myth explains how the Japanese islands were created in history.

The islands of Japan were most likely settled by people migrating from the mainland of Asia. Over a period of many centuries, they developed into a distinctive people, the Japanese. The Ainu, a people entirely different from the Japanese, are the descendants of the earliest settlers of the islands. Only a few thousand have survived. Most Ainu now remain on the northern island of Hokkaido. Japan is one of the world's most closely set populated countries. It accommodates about half the population of the United States. Nearly two-thirds of the Japanese are city slickers, and the number is steadily increasing.

Art and architecture

Japan has a lavish and world-renowned artistic tradition, which encompasses sculpture, textiles, ink painting, calligraphy, ukiyo-e (woodblock printing), and much more. Exquisite kimonos, beautifully painted screens, and images by famous artists such as Hokusai have become famous symbols of the country.

There are a large number of excellent museums where you can admire these creations—from the world's largest collection of ukiyo-e in Matsumoto to the superb Tokugawa Art Museum in Nagoya.

Contemporary art benefits from an excellent standing in Japan, and there are world-class galleries scattered throughout the country.

Japanese architecture, meanwhile, is characterized by wooden structures with sliding paper screens, tatami mats, and curved roofs. Though at first glance, Japanese architecture may seem alike, the Japanese aesthetic is much simpler, cleaner, and less ornate.

Literature

Japanese were greatly influenced by cultural contact with China and Chinese literature, often written in classical Chinese. Indian literature also had an influence through the spreading of Buddhism in Japan.

Japanese literature developed into a distinct style in its own right as Japanese writers began writing their own works about Japan, although the influence of Chinese literature and Classical Chinese existed until the end of the Edo period. Since Japan reopened its ports to Western trading and diplomacy in the nineteenth century, Western and Eastern literature have strongly affected each other and continue to do so.

THE EFFECT OF JAPANESE CULTURE ON THE JAPANESE PERSONA AND TRAITS

Personality

The personality traits most frequently attributed to the Japanese people include politeness, kindness, respectfulness, timidity, intelligence, formality, and a preference for being in groups. The Japanese are also recognized by Westerners as being punctual, hardworking, and neat.

Respectfulness is certainly inherent in Japanese culture. Using informal language with the elder generation who are not related is considered a grave insult.

Formality is tightly associated with respect, and Japanese people tend to err on the side of formal address with foreign friends, unless they are invited to do otherwise.

The importance of punctuality in Japan is also noticeable. Even the slightest delays of trains have been known to leave the whole railway system in chaos.

Work etiquette

In practice, Japanese business etiquette is not dissimilar to that of Europe or the United States—politeness, sensitivity, and good manners are its pillars. The principal difference is that Japanese business etiquette is more formal, especially at a first meeting when the exchange of the infamous Japanese business card is almost ceremonial.

Maybe the most important thing to understand is that the Japanese are very relationship oriented. In Japanese business culture, employees are often hired for a lifetime. This means that there is a mutual understanding that the employee will likely stay with the company for the rest of his or her working life.

In Japanese business etiquette, seating positions are of utmost importance as they are an indicator of status. The highest-ranking position will sit at the head of the table furthest away from the door. The Japanese term for business cards is *meishi,* and foreign visitors are expected to carry them. Bilingual Japanese business cards are a basic minimum requirement for anyone doing business in Japan. When bestowing a business card to your Japanese counterpart, it is expected to use both hands and bow your head slightly while offering the card.

Perception of others

Perhaps the most frequent explanation regarding Japanese miscommunication with foreigners is the fact that Japan is *shimaguni* (an island country). Life on an isolated island 180 kilometers from the closest continental shore has clearly affected the history of Japan by preventing extensive contact with its neighbors. The gaijin complex does not stem from the depth of the Japanese psyche unaided. Some of the aggravation and inconvenience Japanese feel at the presence of foreigners is unquestionably the fault of the latter. In the past foreigners often behaved tastelessly to the Japanese and exhibited an unmistakable air of racial and cultural superiority. Misbehavior by foreigners and their abuse of Japanese docile behavior remain an issue in the Japanese media to this day and not without reason.

Patriotism

Japan may be considered to have the highest sense of pacifism and the lowest sense of patriotism of any country in the world.

Not just the elder generation, but also generations of Japanese who never experienced the war period cannot easily show any love of country. The differences you see in this area between Japan and China, India, Korea, the United States or even Germany are striking.

The guilt that is embedded in the Japanese spirit and causes all generations to avoid signs of patriotism and instead exhibit a strong sense of pacifism comes from a rarely spoken sense of fear. At a basic cultural level, Japanese fear a loss of control. And beginning in the 1920s, a national loss of control led to patriotism turning into nationalism.

Punctuality

It is normal for the Japanese to be punctual. As Japanese are especially concerned about not being late, most have naturally developed this habit. For example, in companies and public institutions and for meetings with others, it is considered common sense to be prompt.

If a train arrives even one minute later than scheduled, Japanese railway companies announce their apologies over the PA. Moreover, *Shinkansen* (bullet train) arrivals and departures are timed within fifteen-second periods.

Six

Introduction to the
Culture of America

US culture has noteworthy regional inflections. Most Americans are aware of these differences despite the fact that these regions have experienced economic transformations and that Americans often abandon their regions of origin.

The Northeast is densely populated. Its extensive corridors of urbanization have been called the national megalopolis. Once a leader in technology and industry, the Northeast has been overtaken in these areas by California's Silicon Valley.

The Midwest is both rural and industrial. It is the home of the family farm and is the corn belt and "breadbasket" of the country. In the Great Lakes area of the upper Midwest, the automobile and steel industries were central to community and economy. As those industries declined, the upper Midwest became known as the rust belt.

The South was defined by its secession from the Union before the Civil War and is correlated with slavery and with subsequent battles over civil rights for African Americans. In contemporary terms, these are the sunshine states, retirement havens, and new economic frontiers.

The West, the last national frontier, is associated with national aspirations and legends of unlimited opportunity and individualism. It has the nation's most open landscapes. California, along with the southwestern states, was ceded to the United States by Mexico in 1848 after the Mexican-American War. The Southwest is distinctive because of its historical ties to colonial Spain, its Native American populations, and its regional cuisine, which has been shaped by Native American and Spanish cultures.

Language

The United States has no official national language. If English is considered its unofficial first language, Spanish is its unofficial second language. The United States ranks fifth in the world in the number of Spanish speakers.

Standard English is the language Americans are likely to speak. Within the social hierarchy of American English dialects, Standard English can be said to be the exemplar of acceptable usage based on the model of cultural, economic, and political leaders. Spoken English includes many dialects that have been influenced by Native Americans, immigrants, and slaves. These languages include not only Dutch; German; and Scandinavian, Asian, and African languages, but also less widely spoken languages such as Basque, Yiddish, and Greek. Thus, spoken English reflects the nation's immigration history.

Religion

The majority of the people are Christian. Catholicism is the largest single denomination, but Protestants of all denominations (Baptist, Methodist, Lutheran, Presbyterian, and others) outnumber Catholics. Judaism is the largest non-Christian faith, followed by Islam, which has a significant African American following. Baptism, the largest Protestant sect, originated in Europe but grew exponentially in the United States, especially in the South, among both whites and blacks. Apart from the many Christian movements from England and Europe that reestablished themselves early in the nation's history, a few religious denominations arose independently in the United States, like the Mormons and the Shakers. Although religion and the state are formally separated, religious expression is an important aspect of public and political life. Almost every president has declared some variety of Christian faith. One of the most significant religious trends in recent years has been the rise of evangelical and fundamentalist sects of the Christian faith. An organized political-religious entity, fundamentalist Christianity significantly influences political agendas.

Seven

The Effect of Culture on the American Persona and Traits

7A. THE CULTURAL IDENTITY OF AMERICA

Ashraf Haggag

Culture

According to the US Census Bureau, the United States is the third largest country in the world with a population of more than 320 million. Because of this, the United States is one of the most culturally diverse countries in the world. Nearly every region of the world has influenced American culture, as it is a country of immigrants, most notably the English, who colonized the country beginning in the early 1600s. US culture has also been shaped by the cultures of Native Americans, Latin Americans, Africans, and Asians.

American culture includes both conservative and liberal elements, as shown by scientific and religious competitiveness, political structures, risk taking and free expression, and materialist and moral elements.

Apart from certain consistent ideological principles (e.g., individualism, egalitarianism, and faith in freedom and democracy), America's geographical scale and demographic diversity have generated a variety of expressions.

Since the late 1970s, the terms "traditional values" and "family values" have become synonymous in the United States, suggesting a congruence with mainstream Christianity. However, family values are arguably a modern subset of traditional values, which is a larger concept. Although it is also not necessarily a political notion, it has become associated with both the particular correlation between Evangelicalism and politics and the broader Christian movement.

Art and architecture

Prior to America's colonization, Native American art prospered in various forms; where the Spanish colonized, Spanish Colonial architecture and the accompanying styles in other media were quickly in place. Early colonial art on the East Coast initially relied on artists from Europe, with John White (1540–c. 1593) the earliest example. In the late eighteenth and early nineteenth centuries, artists primarily painted portraits and some landscapes in a style based mainly on English painting. Furniture makers copying English styles and similar craftsmen were also established in the major cities. In the English colonies, locally made pottery remained resolutely utilitarian until the nineteenth century, with any fancy products imported. The American Revolution produced a demand for patriotic art, especially history painting, while other artists recorded the frontier country. A parallel development taking shape in rural America was the American craft movement, which began as a reaction to the Industrial Revolution.

After 1850 academic art in the European style prospered, and as Americans became more affluent, the flow of European art, new and old, to the United States began; this has continued ever since. After World War II, New York replaced Paris as the center of the art world. Since then many American movements have shaped modern and postmodern art. Art in the United States today covers a wide range of styles.

Architecture in the United States is as diverse as its multicultural society and has been shaped by several internal and external factors and regional distinctions. As a whole it represents a bountiful eclectic and innovative tradition.

Literature

American literature is the literature written or produced in the area of the United States and its former colonies. During its early history, America was a series of British colonies on the eastern coast of the present-day United States. Its literary tradition thus was originally linked to the broader tradition of English literature. However, unique American characteristics and the breadth of its production now represent a separate path and tradition.

THE EFFECT OF AMERICAN CULTURE ON THE AMERICAN PERSONA AND TRAITS

Personality

American society is composed of people from many social, cultural, ethnic, and national backgrounds; different economic situations; and vastly different philosophies of life. Because of this, it is hard to generalize about Americans, although certain traits may seem most obvious to people from other countries.

Probably above all, Americans consider themselves individuals. Although there are strong family ties and strong loyalties to groups, individuality and individual rights are most important. This may seem like a selfish attitude, but it also leads many Americans to an honest respect for other individuals and an insistence on human equality.

Related to this respect for individuality are the American traits of independence and self-reliance. From an early age, children are taught "to stand on their own two feet," or to be independent. Since this is such a marked trait in the American style of relating, you are expected to take care of yourself, and if you do need help, ask for it. Others usually will not offer help until you ask them.

Work etiquette

For a country that prides itself on its individualism, companies are organized and shaped in many different ways, depending on the industry, the company's history, and its current leaders. In the United States, business relationships are formed between companies rather than between people. Americans do business where they get the best deal and the best service. It is not important to develop a personal relationship in order to establish a long and successful business relationship. Americans prefer frankness in communication. When Americans say yes or no, they mean exactly that. When doing business in the United States, it's important to be punctual for meetings. Arriving late is considered rude and disrespectful. Interaction and participation are important during business meetings. If you are quiet and have nothing to say, this can be looked upon as your being unprepared and not having anything to contribute. Meeting deadlines is taken very seriously, and missing agreed-upon deadlines is seen as irresponsible.

Perception of others

Long-established minorities have been living in the United States for long enough (or have grown large enough) to become part of the cultural mainstream. Black Americans, Jewish Americans, and Hispanic Americans score high in the traditional minority dimension. They are generally less disliked and more welcomed in the eyes of white Americans.

Cultural outgroups—atheists, Mormons, and Muslims—are viewed very differently. These groups all fall outside conventional society culturally, behaviorally, or both. White Americans perceive atheists, Mormons, and Muslims through a common lens. They are viewed less favorably and are generally less welcomed than black Americans, Jewish Americans, and Hispanic Americans.

Patriotism

In the United States, patriotism is seen as a fundamental part of American culture. More than half the population owns an American flag, and almost as many own garments with patriotic symbols on it. Phenomena such as flag ownership seem to occur across all generations.

American patriotism is rooted in orthodox values that include honor, loyalty, and bravery, among others; thus, Americans serving in the military and fighting in a war are regarded highly. Joining the military is a reasonable choice for Americans to display their patriotism but also a way to ensure financial stability.

Punctuality

While many other cultures are preoccupied with relationship building, Americans are preoccupied with timekeeping. For Americans, time is almost a tangible asset, which can be saved, spent, lost, invested, and wasted. Their central tenet is that time is money, and wasting time is just as bad as wasting money. Thus, punctuality is an essential part of US business etiquette, and lateness is considered disrespectful and rude. Meetings start on the dot and are expected to proceed uninterrupted. Schedules are important, and deadlines are strictly adhered to. In meetings and negotiations, great emphasis is put on getting the best results in the quickest possible time.

Eight

Introduction to the Culture of the Middle East

The culture of the Middle East has been influenced by many different historical movements and civilizations and is richly diverse, manifold, and intricate. Middle Eastern culture reflects the dichotomy between ancient and modern, traditional and contemporary. Neither the culture nor the cuisine of the Middle East is uniform, and though there are some similarities found throughout the area, culture here varies from country to country and region to region.

Religion

Many aspects of Middle Eastern culture are defined or heavily influenced by religion. Religion is tightly integrated into the cultural institutions of Middle Eastern countries. Islam is the predominant religion in the area, and there are two sects of Islam, Shi'a and Sunni. The two sects have theological and philosophical differences, but they hold the same essential beliefs. A few countries in the Middle East, such as Iran and Iraq, are majority Shi'a, but the majority of those who follow Islam are Sunni. There have been conflicts, both historical and contemporary, between followers of Sunni and Shi'a Islam.

Israel is a Jewish stronghold. Israeli culture differs greatly from that of other Middle Eastern countries because of the Jewish influence. The Middle East also has communities of Christians and practitioners of religions found only in the region. Examples of these are the Druze and Alawites, which started as subtypes of Islam but have developed their own theologies after centuries of adaptation.

Languages

The most extensively spoken language in the Middle East is Arabic. Arabic has several different dialects, and people who speak one version of it fluently may have difficulty understanding and adapting to another version. Despite the differences, the bases for the language are the same, and there is a standard form of Arabic for writing. Arabic is also the language of Islam, as used in the Holy Quran, and many Muslims read and recite holy text in Arabic even if it is not their main language. Persian languages, primarily Farsi, are spoken throughout Iran, and Turkish is spoken in Turkey. The official language in Israel is Hebrew, and most Israeli people speak either Hebrew or English. English and French are spoken among upper-class citizens throughout the Middle East.

Nine

The Effect of Culture on Middle East Persona and Traits

9A. THE CULTURAL IDENTITY OF EGYPT

Culture

The culture of Egypt traces back to thousands of years of recorded history, Ancient Egypt was among the earliest civilizations in all the world and maintained a unique culture, strikingly complex and stable, that influenced later cultures in Europe.

After the Pharaonic Era, Egypt came under the influence of Hellenism, then for a time Christianity, and later Islamic culture.

Plenty has been written, read, debated, and analyzed about the rich culture of Egypt. And yet, the Egyptian culture has remained as intriguing and enigmatic as it was thousands of years ago, guaranteeing an ever-increasing stream of tourists and visitors to the country. Perhaps it has to do with the richness, the treasures, the scientific advancement, the magic, and the colossal architecture—whatever the reason, Egypt and Egyptian culture hold the attention of the world at large.

Art

Egyptian art has been examined and researched by art historians and Egyptologists over the years. The history of art in Egypt dates back to 5000 BC, but the prominence of art, pottery, and paintings can be clearly related to the period from 3000 BC through the fourth century AD.

One of the distinct features of early Egyptian art is its strict adherence to rules and the use of stereotypes. In the depiction of gods, goddesses, and human beings, the ancient Egyptian artist would depict the face in the profile; provide a frontal view of the shoulders, chest, and torso; and paint both feet.

Symbolism is an important aspect of Egyptian art. Symbols conveyed all that could not be expressed otherwise. The use of colors is especially significant in this context. Themes were quite often religious and mythological and very often about the afterlife. Gods, goddesses, animal familiars, and those of royal descent were central to the paintings.

Scenes from mythology and larger-than-life depictions of the Pharaoh were commonly depicted on the walls of tombs, pyramids, obelisks, and temples. Mineral dyes were used, and wood and reed brushes served very effectively to impart a shaded or layered look to the wall paintings.

The ancient Egyptians used papyrus creatively to write and paint. Papyrus picture books and papyrus sheets with elaborate artwork have been discovered by Egyptologists. Pots and earthenware found in tombs, temples, and pyramids testify to the exceptional skill of Egyptians in creatively embellishing these articles. Very often, these pots held the internal organs of the person mummified or were used for ritual purposes.

Architecture
Egypt is best known for its ancient architectural marvels. Think Egypt and the word *pyramids* immediately comes to mind.

The very view of the colossal pyramids and the Sphinx is breathtaking. To acknowledge that these structures were planned and built to perfection more than five thousand years ago, when modern engineering aids were unknown, is simply too magnificent. Ancient Egyptian architecture as evinced in the marvelous temples, tombs, palaces, and obelisks comprises a study in geometric precision and colossal construction. The use of stone distinguished ancient Egyptian architecture. Limestone and granite were used abundantly. Granite was obtained from the stone quarries to the south of Egypt.

Planning was very important. Ground plans and layouts were carefully prepared by the scribes. The use of gridlines is seen in the monument plans discovered by Egyptologists and archaeologists. The use of mortar was unknown. Hence, the stones were carefully cut in the quarries to ensure that they fit well.

Transportation was the next important task. When the Nile was in its inundation cycle, these massive stones were moved in ships built especially for the purpose. An immense labor force, often thousands of men, was hired to build the temples, tombs, pyramids, and palaces. Royal administrators planned the settlements of these laborers as well. Scribes kept account of the payments due them, and the wages were paid in grains, flax, and oil.

Egyptian architects used an elaborate system of pulleys and levers to hoist the stones to form the desired structures.

Once the basic structure was constructed, carving and decoration of the walls was initiated. The construction of tombs and pyramids often lasted throughout the reign of the pharaoh.

Priests were also part of the teams that were formed for construction since they were responsible for casting propitiation spells and overseeing the carving and painting of the walls. The Great Pyramid of Giza, the Sphinx, the Luxor Temple Complex, the Temple Complex of Karnak and the Temple of Horus at Edfu are among the architectural marvels that attract hundreds of thousands of visitors every year.

THE EFFECT OF EGYPTIAN CULTURE ON THE EGYPTIAN PERSONA AND TRAITS

Personality
There is a great segregation between wealthy and influential Egyptians and the rest of the population. This means that relations tend to be more autocratic than democratic between people of different social standing. In terms of the workplace, for example, a subordinate is less prone to question or criticize his or her supervisor. There is no official caste system in Egypt, but it is rare to see members of the upper class socialize with those of the middle and lower classes.

Unlike Western societies that put a value on individualism, Egyptian society focuses on collectivism. An act or decision that benefits the group is better than one that benefits only the individual. It is very common for Egyptians to live in extended families. The emphasis is always on being a good Muslim, family member, worker, and citizen. Loyalty to the community is a highly praised attitude.

Work etiquette
Business is slower in Egypt than in the European working culture, so it is not wise to expect immediate results. Moreover, keeping foreign trade partners waiting is a common practice, and you might not be able to set more than one meeting in one day.

No business is conducted on Friday, the Muslim holy day. When addressing your Egyptian counterparts for the first time, you should use their title followed by their surname until invited to do otherwise. Titles are a sign of stature and are viewed with pride; therefore, it is important to use them. If an Egyptian does not have a title, a courtesy title such as "Mr.," "Mrs.," or "Miss" is appropriate.

Perception of others
Egyptians refer to foreigners as *khawagas*, a term of Persian origin that means *mister* or *respected sir*. *Khawagas* played an important role in the development of Egyptian society.

Opposition to American policies does not translate into hatred of Americans. Another mistake is to interpret Egyptians' struggle against certain forms of capitalist exploitation as a sort of xenophobia. In 1932, for example, the Egyptian author Muhammad Hussein Heikal praised the part played by the *khawagas* in the development of Egypt, even as he criticized excessive foreign ownership of Egypt's resources.

Patriotism

Many Egyptians maintain a well-defined Egyptian identity, and a strong sense of nationalism and patriotism can be noticed even in casual dialogue. Even those in the poorest circumstances cannot help feeling a sense of superiority to their neighbors across the Red Sea.

Most of Egypt's Copts maintain that they have the purest bloodline descended from the ancient Egyptians. Many Egyptians claim that they are Egyptian and of pharaonic descent and the only thing that ties them to the Arabs is the Arabic language.

Punctuality

Punctuality is a relaxed concept in Egypt. It is fine to be thirty minutes late for a social engagement. On the other hand, Egyptians try to make an effort to be on time for foreigners. However, even if your Egyptian business associates arrive late for an appointment, foreign counterparts are expected to be on time.

9B. THE CULTURAL IDENTITY OF TURKEY

Culture

The culture of Turkey incorporates a heavily diverse set of elements that derive from the various cultures of the Eastern Mediterranean, central Asian, Southeastern European, Eastern European, and Caucasian traditions. Many of these traditions were first brought together by the Ottoman Empire, a multiethnic and multireligious state.

During the early years of the republic, the government invested a large amount of resources into fine arts such as painting, sculpture, and architecture, aimed at modernization and the creation of a cultural identity.

Many historical factors define the Turkish identity. The culture of Turkey combines clear efforts at modernization and Westernization, undertaken in varying degrees since the 1700s, with a simultaneous desire to maintain traditional religious and historic values.

Literature

Turkish literature concentrates on the Ottoman court, which produced poetry and prose. This literature represents an amalgamation of Persian, Arabic, and Turkish classical styles. Western influences were introduced in the 1860s by a group of highly developed intellects who attempted to combine Western cultural forms with a more simple form of the Turkish language.

This westernizing trend sustained throughout the nine-teenth century and became more pronounced just before World War I. After 1923, the republic produced an impressive number of novelists, poets, singers, musicians, and artists.

Novelists who gained international fame include Halide Edib, Resat Nuri Güntekin, and, more recently, Orhan Pamuk.

Orhan Veli generally is considered the patriarch of modern Turkish poetry, which is distinguished by a rebellion against rigidly prescribed forms and a preoccupation with immediate perception. Some poets have experimented with obscurantist forms and ideas.

Arts

Western impact on the graphic arts started in the late Ottoman period with the founding of the Fine Arts Academy in Istanbul, operated by European and European-educated Turkish artists.

In the republican periods, Turkish art has included a variety of Western and indigenous styles. Practically all artists of note have studied at the academy or in Europe. Some have imitated European forms, while others have searched for a Turkish style and portray Turkish themes such as village and urban scenes in a representational manner.

Several sculptors received state commissions to create monumental works depicting Atatürk and other patriotic themes. Foreign plays outnumber Turkish works in the theater, but theater attendance has grown substantially in recent decades, and many Turkish playwrights who combine Western techniques with Turkish social issues have had a chance to present their works.

Ankara and Istanbul have music conservatories that encompass schools of ballet. Several Turkish composers, of whom the best known is Adnan Saygun, have won acclaim in Europe and America for fusing Turkish folk themes with Western forms.

The Istanbul Music Conservatory has made steps to preserve authentic folk music by recording it in all parts of the country. Annual folk arts festivals in Istanbul present a wide variety of Turkish music and dance.

THE EFFECT OF TURKISH CULTURE ON THE TURKISH PERSONA AND TRAITS

Personality
The two characteristic traits of the Turkish people are hospitality and family relations.

Hospitality is one of the keystones of the Turkish way of life. Turkish people are the most gracious and generous hosts as a result of their natural instincts. In every corner of the country, traditional hospitality will meet you. Every individual feels bound to honor guests in the best possible manner. They will open their houses to every guest with a smiling face and with all sincerity give the best seat to and cook the best food for their guest. The mentality of that hospitality is "Whatever religion you practice, whichever country you come from, whatever language you speak, you are God's guest, so you deserve to be welcomed in the best manner."

Family relations are very much closed among Turks. They respect the elder generation and support one another in every way. Fathers and mothers support their children financially until they get married. When the child gets married, the financial support may continue, but it is expected that the new family can earn a living. Children take care of their elders and support them, both financially and physically, then they get old or sick. Whereby elders support children when they are young, and children support their elders when they are old.

Work etiquette
Turkish employees work some of the longest hours in Europe, but this isn't always reflected in productivity. The business culture in Turkey allows for a lot of smoking and tea breaks and often prevents employees from acting without explicit orders from above. However, when orders do come, workers are expected to carry them out quite quickly, leading to a stop-start form of working.

Employers expect workers to be time flexible, which sometimes makes it very difficult for women to keep working after they have children. On the other hand, employers in some workplaces, especially those with a strong Islamic ethos, are willing to give their female employees lots of paid time off during pregnancy and lactation.

Turkish people usually do business with those they trust, like, and respect. During greetings, always greet the oldest person first; Turks have a great respect for the elderly. When speaking, it is important to maintain eye contact since this conveys sincerity and helps build a trusting relationship.

Perception of others
Despite the negative inclination of the Turkish public toward world powers, roughly half of them still want to join the European Union. And while many in Turkey remain unhappy with national conditions, there has been a substantial increase in overall life satisfaction there since 2002.

Patriotism
The initial thing you will notice about Turkish people is that they are extremely patriotic and very proud of their ancestors and of the achievements of their modern society. You will notice the Turkish flag proudly displayed everywhere. During Turkish national holidays, including Victory Day, you will see Turkish flags adorn shops, public offices, and houses.

Punctuality

Turkish people are quite traditional and formal when doing business. Therefore, scheduling appointments in advance is important. Furthermore, Turkish people value punctuality and expect international professionals engaging in business with them to do the same. If for some reason you are going to be late, it is essential to call ahead as soon as possible with a reasonable explanation.

9C. THE CULTURAL IDENTITY OF ARABIC COUNTRIES

Culture

Arabic culture refers to the culture of the countries in which the official language is Arabic. Language, literature, gastronomy, art, architecture, music, spirituality, and philosophy are all part of the cultural heritage of the Pan Arab world.

The Arab sphere is sometimes divided into separate regions from the Nile Valley in Egypt and Sudan to North Africa in Libya; from Tunis, Algeria, and Morocco to the Fertile Crescent in Iraq; and from Lebanon, Syria, Jordan and the Arabian Peninsula in south Iraq to Jordan, Kuwait, Bahrain, Qatar, Saudi Arabia, Oman, Yemen and the United Arab Emirates.

The Arab culture is separated into three main parts: the urban culture, the rural culture, and the nomad culture.

The majority of the Arab states of the Persian Gulf, along with parts of Jordan and Iraq, are considered Bedouins. Countrysides in other countries such as Palestine, Syria, Lebanon, Iraq, Algeria, and Tunisia are considered rural cultures. Their major cities like Cairo, Jerusalem, Beirut, Baghdad, Alexandria, Damascus, and so on are considered urban cultures. The Levant, especially Palestine, Lebanon, Syria, and Egypt, has a long urban culture history.

Social loyalty is of utmost importance in Arab culture. Family is one of the most important aspects of the Arab society; Arabic parents teach family loyalty, self-reliance and responsibility to their children. Unlike the extreme individualism we see in North America, Arab society places emphasis on the group. Arab culture teaches that the needs of the group are more important than the needs of one person.

In the Bedouin tribes of Saudi Arabia, intense feelings of loyalty and dependence are fostered and preserved by the family.

One of the characteristics of Arabs is generosity, and they usually show it by being courteous to one another. Among the most important values for Arabs are honor and loyalty. The Arab world is strongly influenced by Islam and its practices, even though not all Arabs are Muslims. In Arab society it is common for a speaker to pepper his or her speech with blessings and proverbs.

Literature

Arabic literature includes the prose and poetry of the Arabic world and is approximately fourteen hundred years old. It has had a vast history, which is manifested by an evolution that originated in native Arabia. This evolution was strongly affected by various external influences that were able to permeate the cloak of the Arab society throughout the existence of Arabic literature.

Arabic literature came to being in the late fifth century, two hundred years before the advent of Islam, in a time known as the

Pre-Islamic period, the Age of Darkness, or the Age of Ignorance because of the absence of Islam. With the help of Islam, Arabic literature progressed from its roots. Despite the fact that they were isolated from foreign cultures, the Arabs were able to develop their literature without help. This shows that Arabic literature owes its early development to the Arabs themselve

The Arabic literary renaissance was the result of the culture's first substantial contact with the East and the West. According to Dale Eickelman, many historians consider Napoleon Bonaparte's expedition to the Muslim Orient in 1978 as very significant in the history of the Middle East, since it forced the Arabs to come face to face with European civilizations, leaving them profoundly affected in many areas.

Modern Arabic literature is the product of fourteen hundred years of evolution. Yet it is not clear what kind of literature it has become. It is still reaping the benefits of its reawakening, which happened just a century ago, which makes it quite young by modern standards. It is still undergoing a transition from the classical period to the modern era.

THE EFFECT OF ARABIC CULTURE ON THE ARABIC PERSONA AND TRAITS

Personality
One of the elements that contributes to the current personality of the Arab nation is the fact that a segment of the

population is impressed with European civilization and the Western lifestyle. They tend to emulate the Western mode of life, believing that this is the way to development and progress. This segment of Arab society is not content with emulating the Western lifestyle; it mocks the Arab personality and its heritage and values. These Arabs alienated themselves from their past and called for the destruction of the Arab cultural and literary heritage. They initiated dubious actions, such as replacing the Arabic characters with Latin ones and using the Arabic dialects instead of standard Arabic. They also began to harp on antiquated regional biases.

Work etiquette

Agendas are likely to be nonexistent. After the traditional five minutes of small talk, business will be brought up and discussed, most likely with the most senior businessman in the room leading and directing the discussion. One of the crucial things to remember when doing business in the Middle East is that many Arabs find it extremely shameful to lose face in public. They will therefore go out of their way to save face, be it their own or that of those around them. Try not to directly disagree with or contradict anyone during a meeting. Telling someone you think he or she is wrong is a sure way of causing the person to lose face, meaning no business deal for you.

Arab, especially those in the Gulf countries, may wear their traditional outfits. These usually consist of a long white robe known as a *thobe* and often a red-and-white-checked headdress called a kaffiyeh. The exact style and color of this dress will vary from country to country, region to region, and even tribe to tribe. Most women in the Gulf dress in the traditional black robe called an abaya and will wear a headscarf. Elsewhere, across the Levant and North Africa, the way businessmen and women dress varies immensely. Some dress traditionally, and others dress in suits or the attire that you would expect to come across anywhere else in the world.

Perception of others
The foreigner complex means that Arabs commend the sayings and deeds of foreign individuals. They trust their qualifications, products, and expertise. This is evidenced by the high demand for foreign-made products, even when such products are produced locally. Furthermore, this complex results in the hiring of foreign experts at very high salaries. It is quite possible that an Arab expert may suggest and idea or propose a project that may not receive a positive response. But, when the same idea is suggested by a foreign expert, it may be hailed by some as a wonderful idea.

Patriotism
Nationalism played a major role in bringing significant changes to the Middle East and the collapse of the Ottoman Empire in 1918. After World War I, Arab nationalism/Pan Arabism emerged in the Middle East. Pan Arabism was a nationalist movement built from the shared heritage of Arabs who lived in lands from the Arabian Peninsula through to North Africa.

During the 1920s and 1930s, violent protests and revolts against Western nations increased turmoil. Additionally, Arab nationalists faced European Zionists in Palestine. While the number of Jews in Palestine dramatically increased, tensions between the Arabs and Jewish community grew as well. As a result, Arab nationalists battled Zionists and other Jews over a land that they called Palestine and the Jews called Israel for the rest of the century.

Punctuality

One significant difference in business etiquette between the Western world and the Arab world is in the attitude toward punctuality. Arab businesspeople generally do not feel the need to be punctual and may even be late on purpose in order to test the commitment of the person with whom they are meeting. However, foreigners are usually expected to be punctual.

Ten

The Elements of Corporate Culture

1. VISION

A great corporate culture starts with a vision or mission statement. These simple words or phrases guide a company's values and provide it with purpose. That purpose, in turn, orients every decision employees make. When they are deeply authentic and prominently displayed, good vision statements can even help orient customers, suppliers, and other stakeholders. Nonprofits often excel at having compelling, simple vision statements.

2. VALUES

A company's values are the core of its culture. While a vision articulates a company's purpose, values offer a set of guidelines for the behaviors and mind-sets needed to achieve that vision.

McKinsey & Company, for example, has a clearly articulated set of values that are communicated to all employees and involve the way that the firm vows to serve clients, treat colleagues, and uphold professional standards.

Google's values might best be articulated by their famous phrase "Don't be evil." But they are also enshrined in its "Ten Things We Know to Be True." And while many companies find that their values revolve around a few simple topics (employees, clients, professionalism, etc.), the originality of those values is less important than their authenticity.

3. PRACTICES

Values are of little importance unless they are enshrined in a company's practices. If an organization professes that people are its greatest asset, it should also be ready to invest in people in visible ways.

Wegman's, for example, heralds values like caring and respect, promising prospects a job they'll love, and it follows through in its company practices; it's ranked by *Fortune* as the fifth-best company to work for.

Similarly, if an organization values "flat" hierarchy, it must encourage more junior team members to dissent in discussions without fear of negative repercussions. And whatever an organization's values, they must be reinforced in review criteria and promotion policies and baked into the operating principles of daily life in the firm.

4. PEOPLE

No company can build a coherent culture without people who either share its core values or possess the willingness and ability to embrace those values. Some of the greatest firms in the world also have some of the most stringent recruiting policies. Great firms are fanatical about recruiting new employees who are not just the most talented but also the best suited to a particular corporate culture. An example at Monster.com: one study found that applicants who were a cultural fit would accept a lower salary, and departments with cultural alignment had less turnover than those without. People stick with cultures they like, and bringing on the right "culture carriers" reinforces the culture an organization already has.

5. NARRATIVE

There is power in narrative. Any organization has a unique history, a unique story. And the ability to unearth that history and craft it into a narrative is a core element of culture creation. The elements of that narrative can be formal—an example is Coca-Cola, which dedicated an enormous resource to celebrating its heritage and even has a World of Coke museum in Atlanta—or informal, like those stories about how Steve Jobs's early fascination with calligraphy shaped the aesthetically oriented culture at Apple. But narratives are more powerful when identified, shaped, and retold as a part of a firm's ongoing culture.

6. PLACE

Why does Pixar have a huge open atrium, engineering an environment where firm members run into one another throughout the day and interact in informal, unplanned ways? Why does Mayor Michael Bloomberg prefer his staff sit in a bull-pen environment, rather than one with separate offices with soundproof doors? And why do tech firms cluster in Silicon Valley and financial firms cluster in London and New York? There are obviously numerous answers to each of these questions, but one clear answer is that place shapes culture. Open architecture is more conducive to certain office behaviors, like collaboration. Certain cities and countries have local cultures that may reinforce or contradict the culture a firm is trying to create. Place—whether geography, architecture, or aesthetic design—affects the values and behaviors of people in a workplace.

There are other factors that influence culture. But these six components can provide a firm foundation for shaping a new organization's culture. And identifying and understanding them more fully in an existing organization can be the first step to revitalizing or reshaping culture in a company looking for change.

Eleven

The Role of Culture in the Corporate Environment

The world is being affected by the globalization of the economy. This phenomenon is bringing intense movement of companies, assets, services, capital, and people.

Analyzing globalization, this process is taking the world through major changes in the economic, technological, and social areas, which has consequences for all organizations and societies that participate in this globalized market.

It is a process that does not bring equal benefits to all participants. Globalization concentrates more of its actions in some sectors of economic activity and some regions and countries, rather than acting everywhere.

Companies from different countries are managed based on distinct values, beliefs, and priorities. Culture directly influences management, producing specific characteristics and forms affecting actions.

The success of an organization is closely related to its capacity for reading, analyzing, and answering the cultural particularities of the region in which it acts. The globalized world intensifies the presence of foreign organizations on all continents, giving more attention to the cultural differences. Culture has an impact on many dimensions of management activity, such as marketing, production, people, and finance and accounting.

In the marketing area, culture influences the tastes, preferences and customs of the consumer. This requires the company to adjust its advertising policies, promotions, product development, location, and pricing to the cultural specifications of the local community.

The area of personnel management is strongly influenced by cultural differences. People's motivations change from one culture to another. Rewards and incentives differ among cultures, obliging managers to adapt their personal management strategies to the local values.

11A. THE INFLUENCE OF CULTURE ON BUSINESS NEGOTIATIONS

International business negotiations do not only cross borders; they also cross cultures. Culture profoundly influences how people think, communicate, and behave. It also affects the kinds of transactions they make and the way they negotiate them.

Differences in culture among business executives (e.g., between a Chinese public-sector plant manager in Shanghai and a Canadian division head of a family company in Toronto) can create barriers that impede or completely thwart the negotiating process.

The great diversity of the world's cultures makes it impossible for any negotiator, no matter how skilled and experienced, to understand fully all the cultures he or she may encounter. How then should an executive prepare to cope with culture when negotiating in London this week and Japan the next?

There are ten elements that consistently arise to complicate intercultural negotiations. These "top ten" elements of negotiating behavior constitute a basic framework for identifying cultural differences that may arise during the negotiation process.

Applying this framework in international business negotiations may assist you in understanding your counterpart better and anticipating possible misunderstandings.

1. NEGOTIATING GOAL—CONTRACT OR RELATIONSHIP?
Negotiators from different cultures may tend to view the purpose of a negotiation differently. For deal makers from some

cultures, the goal of a business negotiation, first and foremost, is a signed contract between the parties. Other cultures tend to consider that the goal of a negotiation is not a signed contract but rather the creation of a relationship between the two sides.

It is therefore important to determine how your counterparts view the purpose of your negotiation. If relationship negotiators sit on the other side of the table, merely convincing them of your ability to deliver on a low-cost contract may not be enough to land you the deal.

You may also have to persuade them, from the very first meeting, that your two organizations have the potential to build a rewarding relationship over the long term. On the other hand, if the other side is basically a contract deal maker, trying to build a relationship may be a waste of time and energy.

2. NEGOTIATING ATTITUDE—WIN-LOSE OR WIN-WIN?
As there can be differences in culture, personality, or both, businesspersons appear to approach deal making with one of two basic attitudes: that a negotiation is a process in which both can gain (win-win) or that it is a struggle in which, of necessity, one side wins and the other side loses (win-lose).

Win-win negotiators see deal making as a collaborative, problem-solving process; win-lose negotiators view it as confrontational. As you enter negotiations, it is important to know which type of negotiator is sitting across the table from you.

3. PERSONAL STYLE—INFORMAL OR FORMAL?
Personal style concerns the way a negotiator talks to others, uses titles, dresses, and interacts with other people.

Culture strongly influences the personal style of negotiators. For example, Germans have a more formal style than Americans. A negotiator with a formal style insists on addressing counterparts by their titles, avoids personal anecdotes, and refrains from questions touching on the private or family lives of members of the other negotiating team.

A negotiator with an informal style tries to start the discussion on a first-name basis; quickly seeks to develop a personal, friendly relationship with the other team; and may take off his jacket and roll up his sleeves when deal making begins in earnest.

Each culture has its own formalities with their own special meanings. They are another means of communication among the persons sharing that culture, another form of adhesive that binds them together as a community. For an American, calling someone by his or her first name is a sign of friendship and therefore a good thing. For a Japanese, the use of the first name at a first meeting is an act of disrespect and therefore bad. Negotiators in foreign cultures must respect appropriate formalities. As a general rule, it is always safer to adopt a formal posture and move to an informal stance if the situation warrants it than to assume an informal style too soon.

4. COMMUNICATION—DIRECT OR INDIRECT?

Methods of communication vary among cultures. Some emphasize direct and simple methods of communication; others rely heavily on indirect and complex methods. The latter may use redundancy, figurative speech, facial expressions, gestures, and other kinds of body language.

In a culture that values directness, such as the American or the Israeli, you can expect to receive a clear and definite response to your proposals and questions. In cultures that rely on indirect communication, such as the Japanese, reaction to your proposals may be seemingly vague comments, gestures, and other signs. What you will not receive at a first meeting is a definite commitment or rejection.

5. SENSITIVITY TO TIME—HIGH OR LOW?

Discussions of negotiating styles invariably include a particular culture's attitudes toward time. It is said that Germans are always punctual, Latins are habitually late, Japanese negotiate slowly, and Americans are quick to make a deal.

Commentators sometimes claim that some cultures value time more than others, but this observation may not be an accurate characterization of the situation. Rather, negotiators may value differently the amount of time devoted to and measured against the goal pursued.

For Americans, the deal is a signed contract, and time is money, so they want to make a deal quickly. Americans therefore try to reduce formalities to a minimum and get down to business quickly. Japanese and other Asians, whose goal is to create a relationship rather than simply to sign a contract, need to invest time in the negotiating process so that the parties can get to know one another well and determine whether they wish to embark on a long-term relationship. They may consider aggressive attempts to shorten the negotiating time as efforts to hide something.

6. EMOTIONALISM—HIGH OR LOW?
Accounts of negotiating behavior in other cultures almost always point to a particular group's tendency to act emotionally.

For example, Latin Americans show their emotions at the negotiating table, while the Japanese and many other Asians hide their feelings. Obviously, individual personality plays a role here as well. There are passive Latins and hot-headed Japanese. Nonetheless, various cultures have different rules as to the appropriateness and form of displaying emotions, and these rules are brought to the negotiating table as well.

Among Europeans, the Germans and English rank as least emotional, while among Asians the Japanese hold that position, but to a lesser degree.

7. FORM OF AGREEMENT—GENERAL OR SPECIFIC?
Whether a negotiator's goal is a contract or a relationship, in almost all cases, the negotiated transaction will be encapsulated in some sort of written agreement. Cultural

factors influence the form of the written agreement that the parties make.

Americans prefer very detailed contracts that attempt to anticipate all possible circumstances and eventualities, no matter how unlikely. Why? Because the deal is the contract itself, and one must refer to the contract to handle new situations that may arise. Other cultures, such as the Chinese, prefer a contract in the form of general principles rather than detailed rules.

8. BUILDING AN AGREEMENT—BOTTOM UP OR TOP DOWN?

Related to the form of the agreement is the question of whether negotiating a business deal is an inductive or a deductive process.

Does it start from an agreement on general principles and proceed to specific items, or does it begin with an agreement on specifics, such as price, delivery date, and product quality, the sum total of which becomes the contract?

Different cultures tend to emphasize one approach over the other. Some observers believe that the French prefer to begin with agreement on general principles, while Americans tend to seek agreement first on specifics. For Americans, negotiating a deal is basically making a series of compromises and trade-offs on a long list of particulars. For the French, the essence is to agree on basic principles that will guide and determine the negotiation process afterward. The agreed-upon general principles become the framework, the skeleton, upon which the contract is built.

9. TEAM ORGANIZATION—ONE LEADER OR GROUP CONSENSUS?

In any negotiation, it is important to know how the other side is organized, who has the authority to make commitments, and how decisions are made. Culture is one important factor that affects how executives organize themselves to negotiate a deal. Some cultures emphasize the individual while others stress the group. These values may influence the organization of each side in a negotiation.

One style is the negotiating team with a supreme leader who has complete authority to decide all matters. Many American teams follow this approach. Other cultures, notably the Japanese and the Chinese, stress team negotiation and consensus decision making. When you negotiate with such a team, it may not be apparent who the leader is and who has the authority to commit the side.

For example, in negotiations in China on a major deal, it would not be uncommon for the Americans to arrive at the table with three people and for the Chinese to show up with ten. The one-leader team is usually prepared to make commitments more quickly than a negotiating team organized on the basis of consensus. As a result, the consensus type of organization usually takes more time to negotiate a deal.

10. RISK TAKING—HIGH OR LOW?
In business negotiations, the negotiators' cultures can affect their willingness to take risks—to divulge information, try new approaches, and tolerate uncertainties in a proposed course of action.

The Japanese, with their emphasis on requiring large amount of information and their intricate group decision-making process, tend to be highly risk averse in negotiations. Americans consider themselves to be risk takers, but an even higher percentage of the French, the British, and the Indians claimed to be risk takers as well.

11B. THE INFLUENCE OF CULTURE ON FORMATION OF BUSINESS STRATEGY
The aim of this section is to indicate the impact of cultural differences on the business strategies of various countries and to show the significance of knowledge about the culture, behaviors, customs, and traditions of a partner country in international business. The two first parts comprise a theoretic essay, in which native cultures are described in the context of international management, and a description of cultural factors that influence the formation of a business strategy. The third part describes the experiences of Young Digital Planet in negotiations and relations with countries of different cultures.

Native cultures and their significance in international management

Globalization and the business activity of large companies all over the world increasingly link various nations and cultures. However, they also reveal profound differences among people and nationalities on the level of communities, individuals, and organizations.

Cultural diversity and coexistence of different cultures in the international business environment requires defining and comprehending the concept of culture itself, as well as classifying cultures according to specific features useful for the business environment.

Religion itself does not affect culture very profoundly. Culture consists of behaviors studied in various situations. The sooner we learn these behaviors, the harder they are to change. A number of factors concerning culture influence the marketing environment—for example, taste depends on cultural conditioning. Culture determines the attitude of different countries toward colors as well. For Muslims, for example, green has a sacred connotation, whereas in Southeast Asia, it is associated with illness. While white is identified with purity in the West, for Asians it is a color of death.

In international corporations, besides specific organizational cultures, national culture differences are a matter of concern. Poles, Germans, Americans, and the French have a different perception of the value of teamwork, a different attitude toward regulations and procedures, and a different perception of time. Considering these differences allows us to +understand the basis of communication, management, or collaboration problems, as well as to decide on a course of action. The fundamental dimensions of national cultures that differentiate us are listed below.

The role of cultural differences

- Attitude toward regulations and principles
- Individualism versus collectivism
- Fragmentary versus holistic perception of the world
- Ascribed status versus achieved status
- Attitude toward time
- Attitude toward environment

Cultural differences or ignorance and nonobservance of the rules and national customs that exist can be frustrating for businesspersons and companies.

A country may break off promising negotiations, cause un-intentional offense to a foreign customer, or commit another social blunder. Therefore, knowledge of the customs and prac-tices applied in international business is of great significance.

Building a business strategy in international management
Business strategy is one of the fundamental instruments of management. The market, economy and creation of an

effective business strategy are the conditions for success. Furthermore, many management failures can be tracked to strategic mistakes.

The concept of strategy is characterized by a diversity of approaches. According to one well-known definition, strategy consists of formulating main missions, intentions, and organizational goals, as well as employing specific policies and indispensable actions to achieve the goals.

Taking the most significant aspects of various definitions, strategy can be characterized as a concept of coherent activity established by company management.

Strategy implementation is guaranteeing the accomplishment of long-term objectives in a chosen domain. The strategy of an organization consists of four fundamental elements:

1. Domain of activity
2. Strategic supremacy
3. Goals to achieve
4. Functional programs

It is essential to focus on the domain of activity. This identifies the market and customers, which determine the company's identity. In international management, market features determine the fundaments of collaboration, and the company's essential task is to adapt different, sometimes contradictory, cultural elements into the corporation's global strategy. The specific cultural elements indicate the fundamental problem of international management.

In adapting philosophy of action and concrete practices to particular countries, management concentrates on developing appropriate formulas for matching products to local market needs. The success of a project is determined by knowledge of its market environment and socio-cultural conditioning.

A company entering a different culture market with its product needs to take various factors into consideration. Suffice to mention such factors as consumer affluence, market absorptiveness, and price level to realize the complexity of the problem. In addition, legal and political conditions, such as tariff walls, nontariff barriers, and legal regulation of products are also of great significance.

Cultural differences are reflected in the awareness of the product (i.e., desired product appearance and features. Knowledge of this subject and its consideration are essential to managing an international business.

Another factor is the religious or native symbolism that we are unfamiliar with. Usage of brand names and symbols ignoring national culture might lead to ambiguities, different perceptions, or incorrect association of a product.

Negotiation and international relations are components of international management, and negotiating is a difficult art. However, it becomes even more difficult when negotiations are carried out between representatives of two different cultures.

Legal, political, or currency systems have a critical impact on the whole process of negotiations and on techniques used. Therefore, the manner of conducting prediscussions with regard to language, cultural context, gestures, and body language is of a great significance. Despite the integration of cultures and languages, gestures are not always unambiguous for people from different parts of the world. While forming an international business strategy, it is also crucial to take gender barriers into consideration. In countries with a hierarchical order, women assume high positions within companies; however, this may be infrequent. In other countries, women are undesirable in the world of business.

A quick example of three different regions that clearly show the differences and the challenges that should be taken into consideration while forming business strategies in different cultures is shown below.

1. Korea
While negotiating with Koreans, it is crucial to remember that Korea is a country of strong Confucian traditions, which

appreciates hierarchism, ceremony, respect for elders, and work etiquette.

The social status of a Korean is determined by ancestry, family social standing, age, professional status, gender, education, and material status. Age is also an important issue in Korean culture. A youthful appearance can be a great obstacle in business. Therefore, people whose age does not imply experience and competence should not conduct negotiations with Koreans.

Women are not as acceptable as their male counterparts in the business field. The native hospitality of Koreans allows them take good care of guests. A clear and strong bond among Korean men and a respect for older and superior male rank and titles are plainly noticeable.

2. Arab countries

Religion has a huge impact on the way Arabians make decisions. It is better to avoid entering into and carrying on negotiations during the month of Ramadan. In most Arab countries, consumption of alcohol and pork is unacceptable. If invited to a common table, one may refuse.

The Arabian negotiation technique is based on an open-door policy, which means that the door to the negotiation room is open to anybody, even people who have nothing to do with the business, which considerably extends the talks.

Arabs dislike haste; therefore, they need time to make a decision. They are geared for consultation rather than confrontation. One should not mention the purpose of the visit or the intention of entering into a contract, leaving the initiative to the hosts.

When negotiating price, Arabs are very hard-line negotiators, so one should be prepared to reduce the opening price. The nuances of nonverbal communication are very important, too.

It is essential to adjust to Arabian customs: when standing, maintain a short distance; never expose shoe soles; and always use the right hand to eat when attending a business dinner invitation. If someone is left-handed, it is acceptable to apologize.

3. United Kingdom
British businessmen, brought up in a monochromatic culture, are mainly focused on the transaction. The British think autonomously, and they are open minded, punctual, and reserved in manner.

The British pay a lot of attention to national equality and the multiculturalism of their country. Another aspect of cooperating with Britain is finance. Being one of the most expensive countries in Europe makes it financially inaccessible to many small companies.

Cultural and social factors are of great importance in international business. A variety of cultures coexist in the global market, and many of them might be entirely new and strange to us.

Every company planning to enter a specific market ought to become acquainted with the culture of the country where they are going to operate; otherwise, the probability of blundering increases. Considering cultural differences and adapting to the partner's actions increase the chances of success with foreign businesspeople.

Behavior is not unimportant to a company's action strategy. A lack of professional training, insufficient knowledge of the history and customs of the country, and relying on improvisation are basic faults of managers. Another factor of success in any region is local market customization. This requires the appropriate organizational structure, as well as thorough knowledge of the market and its customs and cultures.

11C. THE INFLUENCE OF CULTURE ON COMMUNICATION

Culture is one of the factors that determine the way people think, act, and interact, and it is composed of many layers. Some of them are obvious, such as customs, arts, food, and celebrations. Others, such as social status, body language, social interaction, sense of humor, and concept of time aren't as noticeable.

Communicating across cultures is challenging. Each culture has set rules that its members take for granted. Few of us are aware of our own cultural biases because cultural imprinting begins at a very early age. And while some of a culture's knowledge, rules, beliefs, values, phobias, and anxieties are taught explicitly, most of the information is absorbed subconsciously.

The challenge for multinational communication has never been greater. Worldwide business organizations have discovered that intercultural communication is important—not just because of increased globalization, but also because the domestic workforce is growing more and more diverse, ethnically and culturally.

We are all individuals, and no two people belonging to the same culture are guaranteed to respond in exactly the same way. However, generalizations are valid to the extent that they provide clues to what you will most likely encounter when dealing with members of a particular culture.

HIGH-CONTEXT VS. LOW-CONTEXT
All international communication is influenced by cultural differences. Even the choice of communication medium can have cultural overtones. The determining factor may not be the degree of industrialization, but rather whether the country is a high-context or low-context culture.

High-context cultures (Mediterranean, Slav, Central European, Latin American, African, Arab, Asian, and American Indian) leave much of the message unspecified, to be understood through context, nonverbal cues, and between-the-lines interpretation of what is actually said. In contrast, low-context cultures (most Germanic and English-speaking countries) expect messages to be explicit and specific.

SEQUENTIAL VS. SYNCHRONIC
Some cultures think of time sequentially, as a linear commodity to spend, save, or waste. Other cultures view time synchronically, as a constant flow to be experienced in the moment and a force that cannot be contained or controlled.

In sequential cultures (like North America, Britain, Germany, Sweden, and the Netherlands), businesspeople give full attention to one agenda item after another.

In synchronic cultures (including South America, southern Europe, and Asia), the flow of time is viewed as a sort of circle, with the past, present, and future all interrelated. This viewpoint influences how organizations in those cultures approach deadlines, strategic thinking, investments, developing talent from within, and the concept of long-term planning.

Orientation to the past, present, and future is another aspect of time in which cultures differ. Americans believe that the individual can influence the future by personal effort, but since there are too many variables in the distant future, they favor a short-term view. Synchronistic cultures' context is to understand the present and prepare for the future. Any important relationship is a durable bond that goes back and forward in time, and it is often viewed as grossly disloyal not to favor friends and relatives in business dealings.

AFFECTIVE VS. NEUTRAL

In international business practices, reason and emotion both play a role. Which of these dominates depends upon whether we are affective (readily showing emotions) or emotionally neutral in our approach. Members of neutral cultures do not telegraph their feelings but keep them carefully controlled and subdued. In cultures with high affect, people show their feelings plainly by laughing; smiling; scowling; and sometimes crying, shouting, or walking out of the room.

This doesn't mean that people in neutral cultures are cold or unreceptive, but in the course of normal business activities, neutral cultures are more careful to monitor the amount of emotion they display. Emotional reactions were found to be least acceptable in Japan, Indonesia, the United Kingdom, Norway, and the Netherlands and most accepted in Italy, France, the United States, and Singapore.

Reason and emotion are part of all human communication. When expressing ourselves, we look to others for confirmation of our ideas and feelings. If our approach is highly emotional, we are seeking a direct emotional response: "I feel the same way." If our approach is highly neutral, we want an indirect response: "I agree with your thoughts on this."

When it comes to communication, what's proper and correct in one culture may be ineffective or even offensive in another. In reality, no culture is right or wrong, better or worse—just different. In today's global business community, there is no single best approach to communicating with one another. The key to cross-cultural success is to develop an understanding of, and a deep respect for, the differences.

11D. THE INFLUENCE OF CULTURE ON CREATIVITY AND INNOVATION

Creativity is a powerful catchword. In Western societies, it epitomizes success, the modern trends of novelty and excitement. Whether linked to individuals, enterprises, cities, or regions creativity establishes immediate empathy and conveys an image of dynamism. Creativity is a positive word in a society constantly aspiring to innovation and progress.

The objective is to have a better understanding of the influence of culture on creativity, a motor of economic and social innovation. Do music, visual art, cinema, and poetry, for instance, contribute to creativity in a way that stimulates job creation, economic prosperity, learning, and social cohesion? What is the impact of artistic creation on innovation? Why do companies want to be associated with culture and art? What is the social function of artistic and cultural creativity?

CULTURAL INFLUENCE ON INNOVATION

Innovation plays an important role in developing the economy, expanding and sustaining firms' performance, maintaining a competitive edge in the industry, improving the standard of living, and creating a better quality of life.

Culture influences the behavior of employees, which paves the way to accepting innovation as a significant asset of the firm as well as allowing employees to feel more committed to their organization. Talented employees are valued company assets, which enables them to give an extraordinarily high performance in a particular area that demands some specific skills and training.

The emergence of talent is always associated with two very important environmental factors: education and training. Business leaders are well aware of the fact that the success of their businesses is heavily dependent on the optimum use of potential employees. Those who are inclined toward learning and receptive to environmental changes are well equipped to utilize their potential.

Culture-based innovations require the following:

- Personal abilities (ability to think laterally or in a non-linear way and to be imaginative)
- Technical skills (often artistic skills or craftsmanship)
- Social environment (a social context through education that encourages and appreciates innovations as

well as an economy that invests in culture and culture-based innovations.

CULTURE AND INNOVATION

Cultural productions, as communication tools charged with subjectivity and emotion, have been part of the expression of social life since the origin of humankind. Culture-based creativity plays a key role in generating social innovation.

Art and culture can benefit public service delivery and innovation in a variety of ways:

1. Public service broadcasters are an example of this, and many make much of their reputation as trusted media providers.
2. Participation in cultural activities can emphasize a feeling of belonging in society, which also increases trust in the public realm and public services. Culture can, therefore, help bring certain public services closer to their constituents.
3. Some public services have pioneered new methods of collaborative feedback and decision making by means of integrating creative media innovations—online discussion forums, social networking sites, and online petitions allow the public to interact more easily with public services.
4. Some public services promote participation and involvement, often of marginalized groups.

The development of community media and community arts more generally are good examples of this.

- Culture contributes to strengthening social ties among communities and thereby nurtures individual as well as organizational self-esteem and, ultimately, well-being.
- Social cohesion can be defined as a set of shared norms and values for a society that also encompasses the diversity of people's backgrounds and helps ensure that those from different backgrounds have similar life opportunities. Cultural activities can help express specific cultures while also developing strong and positive relationships among people from different backgrounds in the workplace, in schools, and in neighborhoods.
- Culture can offer new approaches to tackling social problems for which current approaches are deemed inadequate. Policy areas in which culture has successfully helped in this respect include urban regeneration, social cohesion, crime prevention, health, and the fight against pollution.

11E. THE INFLUENCE OF CULTURE ON EMPLOYEES

Company culture can be described as an organization's brand or personality; it's what you believe in and stand for and what makes your company unique. Company culture has everything to do with how employees, prospective employees, customers, and the public perceive your organization.

Company culture is powerful. It can impact sales, profits, recruiting efforts, and employee morale, both positively or negatively. A great company culture attracts people who want to work for or do business with a company.

It can inspire employees to be more productive and positive at work while reducing turnover. It can even act as your best recruiter, attracting qualified candidates who want to work for your company. It's easy to see how important company culture can be.

Below are the three aspects of company culture's impact on employees.

1. Impact on employee performance
Company culture impacts individual performance. To provides the biggest competitive advantage, an organization's culture must be strong and widely communicated and reinforced. Everyone must share its values and beliefs.

In a strong-culture company, employees enjoy at least some control over their jobs, instead of feeling powerless. Whether it's by working from home, choosing their projects, or trying out new roles, employees who feel valued and can make decisions achieve a higher level of performance.

Strong company cultures also give employees opportunities to grow. Offering promotions, career development programs, or extra training can keep employees motivated—which in turn improves performance. When everyone is in it together, they will all put forth the extra effort to achieve organizational goals.

2. Impact on employee happiness

A positive company culture can ensure that employees remain satisfied with their jobs and loyal to the organization. This can be extremely beneficial in a competitive hiring environment. People are much more interested in signing on (and staying) with a company culture that promotes flexibility, supports employee development, and offers work-life balance.

Improving employee satisfaction through a strong and supportive company culture can reduce recruiting, hiring, and training costs while improving morale and increasing profits.

3. Impact on employee engagement

Now, it is clear that a strong company culture has quite an impact on employee performance and satisfaction. Here are some ways that company culture can impact employee engagement:

- Communication: In companies with good communication practices, employees know their opinions, and ideas are welcomed. When employees feel heard, they don't carry the resentment that can lead to absenteeism, negative morale, and termination. A communicative company culture also leads to greater participation, creativity, and innovation.

- Safety: Organizations that value employees emphasize safety. When safety becomes ingrained in a culture, employees are more mindful and engaged when performing their duties.
- Collaboration: Rather than an "us versus them" approach, collaborative companies promote autonomy, decision making, and teamwork. Employees are given opportunities to contribute, placed in roles in which they can succeed, and offered opportunities to build meaningful relationships with managers and coworkers.
- Growth: Cultures that foster employee development and growth give workers something to work toward and look forward to. Such cultures prevent boredom and job stagnation while keeping things exciting and interesting.

11F. THE INFLUENCE OF CULTURE ON CONSUMER BUYING BEHAVIOR

The process of human consumption, which has been present from the beginning, was initially an activity that had be fulfilled for life, whereas today, it has become the goal of life.

Consumption that is not due to the needs of consumers but in accordance with the wishes of consumers is an evolving process. In terms of marketing, it has become necessary to examine the aspects of consumer behavior that remain in order to define their influence. Concepts such as culture, subculture, social class, and how to influence consumers' buying behavior have been studied.

A consumer is a person who desires or needs marketing components in his or her capacity as a buyer.

Typically, marketers are thought to have the ability to control customers' behavior, but actually, they have neither the power nor the information to do so. A marketer may influence buying behavior but does not control it. Marketers can only influence the consumer by showing how the product or service will be beneficial to the consumer. There are other factors that the marketer cannot control, such as the consumer's culture, profession, attitude, and past experience.

The effect of culture on consumer behavior
International marketers believe that consumers increasingly resemble each other, and they will eat the same food and wear same clothes.

To trade in international markets, marketers must overcome the large cultural and economic boundaries. To improve competition in the worldwide market, they must also understand different traditional beliefs, preferences, habits, and customs.

Culture involves a society's thoughts, words, traditions, language, materials, attitudes, feelings, and beliefs. The beliefs of the people in a community can show similarities. For example, the number four is considered unlucky in Japan; because of that, most products are sold in groups of five. Another element of culture, tradition, is related to the non-verbal behavior of individuals. In France the men use more cosmetic products than the women, which shows the self-conscious tradition of the French men. Cultural properties have been important variables in the analysis of consumer behavior, especially in market segmentation, target markets, and product positioning.

Subculture
Another important concept that should be examined in terms of marketing management is subculture: culture and behavior of individuals with similar values form smaller groups.

The effect of subculture on consumer behavior
Geographical regions and religions are essential in the formation of subculture. The preferences of individuals who live very close to one another can be different. Individuals belonging to different groups have different subculture values, attitudes, and social structures. These differences and subcultural segmentation of market activity have been important variables. It is important to know the characteristics of the subculture in creating the marketing mix price, brand name identification, promotional activities, and product positioning.

Social class

There are several features of social class. First, the behavior, education levels, attitudes, values, and communication styles of members of a social class structure are similar, and these characteristics are different from those of members of other social classes.

The effect of social class on consumer behavior

Social classes are relatively homogeneous and continuous groups who share similar values, interests, and behaviors. Social classes pronounce preferences in clothing, home furnishing, entertainment, and gaming activities, such as automobiles and certain products and brands. Some marketers focus their efforts on only one social class. Social classes are also different in their choice of media. Upper-class consumers prefer books and magazines while lower-class consumers prefer television. As for TV programs, upper-class consumers prefer news and dramas, while lower-class consumers prefer films and sports programs. There are also language differences among social classes. Advertisers should be prepared with the language that is spoken by the social class.

Twelve

Conclusion

Culture in today's context is different from the traditional, more singular definition. Culture is the beliefs, values, mind-sets, and practices of a group of people. It includes the behavior pattern and norms of that group—the rules, the assumptions, the perceptions, and the logic and reasoning that are specific to a group.

Culture is really the collective programming of our minds from birth. It's this collective programming that distinguishes one group of people from another. Much of the problem in any cross-cultural interaction stems from our expectations.

The problem is that whenever we deal with people from another culture—whether in our own country or globally—we expect people to behave as we do and for the same reasons. Culture awareness most commonly refers to having an understanding of another culture's values and perspective. This does not mean automatic acceptance; it simply means understanding another culture's mind-set and how its history, economy, and society have impacted what people think. Understanding so you can properly interpret someone's words and actions means you can effectively interact with them.

When talking about culture, it's important to understand that there really are no rights or wrongs. People's value systems and reasoning are based on the teachings and experiences of their culture. Rights and wrongs then really become perceptions. Cross-cultural understanding requires that we reestablish our mind-set and, most importantly, our expectations, in order to interpret the gestures, attitudes, and statements of the people we encounter. We reestablish our mind-set, but we don't necessarily change it.

There are a number of factors that create a culture—manners, mind-set, rituals, laws, ideas, and language, to name a few. To truly understand culture, you need to go beyond the lists of dos and don'ts, although those are important too. You need to understand what makes people tick and how, as a group, they have been influenced over time by historical, political, and social issues. Understanding the "why" behind culture is essential.

When trying to understand how cultures progress, we look at the factors that help determine cultures and their values. In general, a value is defined as something that we prefer over something else—whether it's a behavior or a tangible item. Values are usually acquired early in life and are often not rational—although we may believe that ours are actually quite rational. Our values are the key building blocks of our cultural orientation.